Memoirs Of A Sai Student

By

Aravind Balasubramanya

I0086341

Publications Division

PRASANTHI NILAYAM

SRI SATHYA SAI SADHANA TRUST,
Publications Division
Prasanthi Nilayam - 515 134
Anantapur District, Andhra Pradesh, INDIA
STD: 08555 ISD: 91-8555 Phone: 287375 Fax: 287236
E-mail: orders@sssbpt.org

ISBN: 978-93-5069-058-1

First Edition: October, 2013, **Reprint**: December, 2013
Revised Edition: February, 2014

Published by

The Convener,
Sri Sathya Sai Sadhana Trust, Publications Division
Prasanthi Nilayam, India, Pin Code - 515134
STD : 08555 ISD: 91-8555   Phone: 287375 Fax: 287236

Printed at
Createspace

Publisher's Note

Bhagawan Sri Sathya Sai Baba is the embodiment of pure and selfless love. His love towards His students is boundless. He told that students are His real property. The experiences, which students in His colleges had with Him, were unique, intimate, and spiritually transforming.

Sri. Aravind Balasubramanya, as a student, Bhagawan loved and moulded him to become a good speaker, writer, and a service-oriented person. In this very interesting, absorbing, and spiritually enlightening book, titled 'Memoirs Of A Sai Student', Sri Aravind describes his unique experiences with his Divine Master in a simple and lucid style.

The Publications Division of Sri Sathya Sai Sadhana Trust has great pleasure to present this book to the devotees, general readers, and student community in particular and hopes that it will be received well.

Date: 27th September, 2013   **Convener**
Prasanthi Nilayam

Table Of Contents

Foreword

"People feel that My property consists of all these lands and buildings... But let Me tell you, My students are My only property. I have given Myself to them." - Baba

To become a part of 'His property' is the most sublime dream, a proud privilege and in fact the greatest good fortune for any child of Sai. However, He has often reminded us -

"Sai's students are those who follow Sai's teachings and strive to make their lives His message."

In that sense all of us have the opportunity to become 'His students' and hence 'His Property'.

However, the greatest transcendental moments of life happen when these two things happen together – being a student in Swami's school and His college and being 'His student'. The magic of His physical presence in our lives can alter the very DNA of our destinies. When the Chancellor of the universe becomes the Chancellor of our university, education becomes for life and not just for a mere living.

His walk, His word, His act, His look, His smile... whether in waking or in a dream are verily the panacea for a thirsting and aspiring soul. That divine impression can never be adequately captured in mere words of language and ink. But today, when the physical form of the Avatar has become one with the Universe, words are the only respite we have. However, when those moments are narrated with a persuasive, passionate and imaginative pen, they can recreate some of that magic.

This book does precisely that. When you read the anecdotes recorded by brother Aravind, you will be able to truly appreciate the narrative style that he has used to relive that Divine Magic along with the nectarine experience that the Lord showers on His students. Through each chapter you will notice that brother Aravind has so wonderfully painted the background, conveyed the facts, concretized the emotions, and doled out the message and impressions - all blended into one seamless narration, a gift that he has received in abundance from Bhagwan.

I have been extremely privileged to not only read all these wonderful memoirs but also be a part of some of these stories as and when they happened. I invite the readers to forget their mundane occupations and dive deep into this ambrosial nectar which conveys the story of a mother and her child, a father and his son, a loving god and his devotee, a caring master and his student, find themselves in these stories and pick out the gems of wisdom and grace which will help in our ultimate journey towards Him.

Amey Deshpande

About The Author

Aravind Balasubramanya hails from a family that has been devoted to Bhagawan Sri Sathya Sai Baba for nearly half a century. His father was a photographer of Bhagawan in the late sixties and early seventies in Brindavan and many of the old black and white photographs we see of Swami have have been through his lens.

Inspired by his parents, especially his mother, to spend his life with his Swami, Aravind joined Sri Sathya Sai Vidyapeeth in Calicut, Kerala for his primary education. He joined Sri Sathya Sai Higher Secondary School in Prashanti Nilayam for high-schooling. He followed it with a Bachelors in Science with specialization in Chemistry from the Sri Sathya Sai Institute of Higher Learning for which he secured a gold medal. He continued to complete his Masters in Science (Chemistry) and with the desire to stay with Bhagawan went on to do his Masters in Business Administration (MBA) too.

It was in the Institute that he got several opportunities to speak in the Divine Presence, act in many presentations and plays and also pursue photography which he picked up from his father. He was careful in recording almost every day that he spent in the physical proximity of his Lord via his many personal diaries and photographs.

Blessed by Baba to join Radiosai Global Harmony, which has been singly responsible in spreading the message and life of Bhagawan to all parts of the globe, he currently does a host of activities there including the Thursday Live satsangs, producing documentaries on Swami and his message and, of course, writing articles.

He was Swami's 'official' photographer for nearly 5 years and travelled along with Him during His trips to Hadshi, Mumbai, Delhi and Simla. Photography is not just his hobby - it's his passion and he has worshipped Swami through it. After Bhagawan's Mahasamadhi in April 2011, Aravind started to write blogs based on what he had recorded in his personal diaries and experiences of several students. The blogs hit a million views and, based on feedback from readers, he was inspired to contemplate a book.

More than all this Aravind has tremendous love for Swami, his biggest and greatest hero. That's what propels him to excel in any and all endeavors that he takes up - be it writing, speaking, photography or video editing.

Acknowledgements

I offer this book to my beloved Swami – my best friend and Master. He gave me the wonderful chance to live with Him as His student in school and University. He blessed me with the good sense to write down the happenings during my student life on a daily basis. Finally, He also gave me His word that the more I share about Him, the more I shall receive from Him. That was the inspiration for me to start blogging actively , which I continue to do at http://aravindb1982.hubpages.com and at http://aravindb1982.blogspot.in.

Very often I received mails and messages from several readers asking me why I wouldn't write a book. I am convinced that it was Swami through so many readers who instructed and inspired me to compile the articles into this book. It is He who is present in every page of this book just as He is in every page of the book of my life. I am also grateful to Him for sending me a host of His instruments to make this intimate book, a reality.

My wife Pooja Aravind Digumarti and Sai-sister Shalu Chandiramani helped to go through the book and make the text error free and grammatically right. My sister and best critic, Shruti Mahadevan, was there to give suggestions on every aspect of the book. My brother Amey Deshpande has been an integral part of the narratives in this book and he has been an inspiration for me in both, storytelling and loving Swami. My colleagues C G Sai Prakash and Ajish Mohan helped in designing a beautiful cover for the book for which Jaidev Kesavan did the page layout. It was Sai-brother Nitin Acharya who enthusiastically took up the project of getting the book printed by the Books and Publications division of the Sri Sathya Sai Sadhana Trust.

I would be doing a grave mistake if I forget to mention the inspiration my parents have been for me - not only in writing about

Swami, but also in guiding me to hold on to His feet throughout my life.

Last but not the least, I must thank you, dear reader, for what is a book without a reader? Your thoughts and feelings are most valuable to me and I consider the reader's feedback and mail as messages to me from my Swami. You can write to me at aravindb1982@gmail.com.

Aravind Balasubramanya
(Prasanthi Nilayam)
31st August 2013

Chapter 1

How Bhagawan Sri Sathya Sai Baba Became My Family Deity

A Different Kind Of Veni Vidi Vici

It was Julius Caesar who mentioned the immortal words - *Veni Vidi Vici* after a short war in the city of Zela in modern day Turkey. He summarized the war very simply - "I came, I saw, I conquered." When it comes to stories of people who have come to Bhagawan Sri Sathya Sai Baba and become His staunch devotees, one is reminded of these very words of Caesar. This is because, if everyone were to summarize their story into 6 words like Caesar did, they would be "I came, I saw, He conquered" - as simple as that.

It is indeed the fulfilment of destiny and the good fortune of many previous births that one gets the chance to live life under a Master's guidance. For my family, the Lord who has been guiding us has been Bhagawan Baba. And just like everyone else, who has a fantastic story of how he/she was introduced to Him, I too have a story of how our family was introduced to Him. But before I start delving into that beautiful story, I must say one thing about coming to a Master.

If one thinks that one arrived at a Master, one cannot be more wrong! It is always the other way round. Whenever a person is ready for his/her spiritual growth, the Master personally invites him/her. And this invitation can come in many ways – as a great tragedy, a miracle, an inexplicable series of coincidences or even a sudden sense of attraction. One thing is for sure - the person who has received the 'invite' knows beyond doubt that it is indeed something very special and divine.

The Strange Haridasa Is, In Fact, Hari!

The short story that I am about to narrate dates back to the September of 1963. The opening sequence is set in the large family home of my grandfather, which was located in Vyalikaval, Bangalore. My father was a bonny lad, 11 years of age then, while his eldest brother (my father is the youngest of six children) was 31 years old and in his working prime. He was working as a stenographer in the Tata Oil Mills Company TOMCO).

One night, as my uncle slept peacefully, he had a very strange dream. He saw a *Haridasa* with his bull. In Karnataka, Andhra Pradesh and many other states of India, there is a tradition where a person moves along the streets with a decked and decorated bull. He often carries a *shehnai* (a wind instrument) on which he plays melodies, singing the glory of God. His job is to remind the society, in its day-to-day life, about God. In return, the society sustains him by giving him alms and food. That is why he is called the *Haridasa* or the servant of Lord Hari. The *Haridasa* in my uncle's dream, however, was very strange. He was short, wore a saffron robe and had a thick mop of curly hair. He placed his hand on my uncle's head in benediction. Thus, my uncle received the first sign of grace, his 'calling' from his going-to-be Lord.

When he woke up the next morning, the dream was fresh and vivid in his memory but he did not pay any extra attention to it. Days turned to weeks and weeks turned to months - the dream was soon forgotten.

The Startling 'Chance Discovery'

The *Haridasa*, however, came thumping back into my uncle's life in a very 'coincidental' manner. He was riding his two-wheeler on his way back home. As he passed by the Seshadripuram police station, he noticed that there was a small *pandal* fabricated tent structure) erected at the nearby Rama temple. At this small shrine dedicated to Lord *Kodanda* Rama (Rama with His bow), there was a gathering of 40-50 people and someone seemed to be addressing them. Even as he was riding past, he bent down to see who the speaker was."

He almost fell off his vehicle! The speaker there was the same *Haridasa* who had come in his dream months earlier! It was the December of 1963 and Swami was on a visit to the city of Bangalore. (He was a frequent tourer then, visiting more than 500 villages and towns in Andhra Pradesh and Karnataka.) My uncle got off the vehicle and stood listening to what the *Haridasa* was saying. Today, he does not remember what He was speaking but he was simply mesmerized and awestruck at this strange coincidence. What were the chances of seeing some stranger in a dream and meeting the exact same stranger months later?

Swami Enters The Home...

My uncle made enquiries and found out that this 'Swami' was the Sai Baba of Puttaparthi, a reincarnation of the Sai Baba of Shirdi. Somebody there gave him a small photograph of the Swami. The coincidence was so powerful that he simply took the photograph and placed it in the altar, next to a picture of Shirdi Sai Baba. Thus the Lord entered the home in the form of a picture. It was now time to 'enshrine' Himself in the hearts of this family. How that happened is another small but interesting episode, which I must mention.

In the year 1964, when curiosity got the better of him, my uncle decided to make a visit to Puttaparthi. And he decided to take along with him, his youngest brother - my father. After traveling for ten tedious hours, they reached Puttaparthi and were in time for the *Dassara* (Hindu festival of celebrating the victory of good over evil) celebrations. They were amazed at the crowds that had gathered there. A few thousands were there! (Little did they know then that the number of devotees would swell beyond millions in the future!)

They also got a chance to hear many stories of Grace and Love of Swami. After staying there for a day or two, they returned to Bangalore.

A few months later, my uncle got a transfer order from his office. He had to pack up and leave for Calcutta (present day Kolkata). He was not at all happy because he did not want to leave his family and ancestral home. He tried everything possible to avoid the transfer but the only alternative offered to him was to the leave the company. Not knowing what to do, he decided to 'try out' this new 'Swami' who promised miracles. All alone, he set out to Puttaparthi. Reaching there, he sat in the *darshan* (physical sight or vision as bestowed by the Master in conglomeration) grounds hoping to get an interview.

Swami Enters The Heart, And Stays There For Life...

Getting an interview with Bhagawan those days was a real easy thing. Devotees say,"If one stayed in Puttaparthi for four days, one was assured of an interview." (God how I wish those days return!)Soon enough, my uncle got an interview. He was planning to stand and ask this 'tiny 'Swami' whether he could help cancel his transfer, at least for that year. However, his experience inside the interview room was overwhelming.

At first sight, he simply fell at Swami's feet. Swami patted him on the head, just as He had done so in his dream more than a year ago! Then, He told him lovingly, "You are worried so much about your transfer right?" So eager was my uncle to get the problem solved that he actually missed noticing Swami's omniscience about his problem. Even before he could open his mouth, Swami said, "Don't worry. You will stay in Bangalore only. Is there anything else you want to ask?" My uncle was tongue tied.

Swami tells us often, "I give you what you ask for so that one day you will ask for what I have come to give you." Sadly, that day somehow never seems to come! We just are tongue-tied when Swami grants us what we ask for, without us asking for it!

Today, my uncle is in his 80s. It is almost 50 years since that interview. My uncle retired at the stipulated age of 58 from TOMCO and to this day, he has not moved out of Bangalore! By promising him that he would never move out of Bangalore, Swami moved into his heart forever. Using him as an instrument, Swami moved into the hearts of everyone else in the family. I shall stop with saying this much that the December of 1963 is a period in time for which I shall be eternally grateful. It sowed the seeds of love for Swami in a family, into which I got the chance of being born.

**Swami posing for a photograph,
as desired by my father on his birthday.**

Chapter 2

How Swami Became My God - My Childhood Experiences With Sri Sathya Sai Baba

'Unanswerable' Questions...

There are some things in life for which we can never find an answer. After experiencing the Love and Grace of Swami, I have discovered many such questions for which, nobody can ever provide a satisfactory answer. Some of these are: "All are equal in the eyes of God. Why then do some people seem 'blessed' while others seem 'less-blessed'?" "At what point in time does the Lord enter one's life?" "Why does Swami do the things that He does?" This is not any attempt to delve into those questions. For now, it is best to leave these questions unanswered. However, one would have to admit, when Swami does enter one's life or confers an experience, one just cannot miss it. Swami comes into one's life with all the Love, Grandeur, Majesty, Grace and Omnipresence that one is simply awe-struck.

I remember my father telling me once, "People get possessed by ghosts. It is our good fortune that we have been possessed by God. Our lives are sanctified for He will never leave us. If a mere 'ghost' has so much powers of possession, imagine how powerfully the Lord will be able to do the same!"

The narration that follows next, is to re-live some interesting episodes. It is through these that Swami entered my life and became the centre of it, (thus, convincing me of His Divinity). There are three distinct episodes from my childhood that I remember clearly.

Episode 1 - Pre-emptive Divine Action In Dream

I was introduced to Swami when we were staying in Bangalore. Later, we moved to Mumbai. I had few *Darshans* of Swami by then and those were enough to instil in me, love and devotion for Him. I had made a small altar for Him on the cornice board above a window in my room. I used to climb onto a table using a stool and then place flowers in worship on His photograph.

One night, I had a dream in which, Swami was walking with my mother on a road when I caught up with them. Swami turned suddenly and held my right wrist. He held it very tight but did not speak anything. After a while, He let go of my wrist and told me to go back. I returned and He continued to walk along with my mother. I woke up.

This was the first time I had a dream about Swami. I felt that somehow it had some inner meaning. Today I know that all dreams of Swami are true. I didn't then! So, I went and narrated the dream to my parents. They too must have been surprised because such things had not happened in our family thus far. We were only "a couple of months old" in 'Sai's fold', as it is called. But both of them were very happy that I had the dream.

In the morning, after I finished my bath, according to my daily schedule, I climbed up the table to place flowers for Swami at His altar. Even as I was placing flowers, unknown to me, my sister came and took the stool away. She wanted to clean the ceiling fan, standing on the stool.

Out of sheer force of habit, I simply stepped back from the table so as to land on the stool. But the stool was not there! Needless to say, I had a fall. I fell straight on my right hand and my right wrist was in severe pain. My parents thought that I had broken my wrist. I was hurried to a doctor who said, "You are lucky young fellow! You did not suffer any fracture. Just rest your wrist for a day and it should be fine."

On the way back home, all of us were discussing my dream that morning with great joy and excitement. That was the first time I closed my eyes and thanked Swami. My love for Him grew and my faith in Him was strengthened. His love for me was like that of a mother - no wonder He was with my mother in that dream!

Episode 2 - God Is Always Watching

*The picture of Bhagawan that adorned
the wall next to the television*

The cable TV in general and the Star TV network in particular were the 'upcoming and happening' things in India, in 1991-92. It was the beginning of the age of "addictive television" to which Swami refers as **Tele Visham** (poison transmitted through the telly). I had acquired a craze for watching WWF - freestyle wrestling - from my friends. (WWF later changed to WWE when the World Wide Fund for nature protested against using the same letters and misleading people) It was what they discussed during the recess in school. There were hundreds of WWF card games and board games. Each of us had our 'heroes' whom we would want to watch.

My mother was not at all happy with this and rightly so. She told me that I should stop watching such violent stuff. I pleaded to her to let me watch for about half an hour everyday but it was to no avail. One day, I sensed a superb opportunity.

My mother had slept in the afternoon. My father had gone to office and sister was in school. The time was 2:30pm - WWF would be starting on Star Sports any moment now. I got tempted. I slowly closed my mother's bedroom door. Then, I went to the television and brought the volume slider (it was a manual slider in TVs of that age) to zero. I then went to flick the main switch on. Little did I know that Swami knows my thoughts even as they arise!

When my finger touched the switch to put it on, something hit me on my hand. I was shocked and instinctively withdrew my hand. I was wondering what it was that had hit me. When I saw, it was a huge marigold flower that had been placed on Swami's photograph which was also on the same wall as the switch. The photo featured Swami looking directly with an all-knowing smile. I got very scared. I felt Swami was telling me, "I am watching always."

I did not switch on the television - nor did I watch WWF after that. As soon as my mother woke up, I went to her, hugged her and narrated the whole episode. She simply smiled and hugged me back.

That day, I realized that God was not just Mother's Love but also Father Discipline.

Episode 3 - Swami Takes Care Even Before We Pray For His Intervention

This was another dream experience that followed close in heels to the above two. By now, we were convinced as a family that Swami was the all-powerful and all-loving Lord, taking care of us always. At this point in time, I had a dream in which, Swami advised me not to go to school the next day.

When I woke up in the morning, the first thing I did was to tell my parents that I would not be going to school as Swami had told me not to go to school. My mother was in a doubt. Here was a perfectly normal and healthy boy telling that he would not go to school. But he was also saying that Swami said so. Is he 'using' Swami to his advantage because he has some other plans for today? She asked me, "Did Swami really tell you not to go to school?" That was a tone and look to which I could never lie in my life! But, I had no need to lie now! "Yes! He told me not to go to school," I replied very confidently. That was enough to convince my mother and make my sister feel very jealous! The same day, within a few hours of having breakfast, I developed a fever. The temperature rose higher and by the afternoon, I had been diagnosed with chickenpox! Once more, we just offered our gratitude to Him.

Returning to the questions asked in the beginning of the article, I am now convinced that I need not know every answer. And that is because there are no 'right answers' - only 'right questions'! The answer for my heart is that everything that happens is for the good alone. And with that answer, I have lived so far - I am sure I'll live happily ever after too because Swami has said that it is such acceptance of everything as good for one which constitutes true surrender.

Chapter 3

The PUSH Of The Lord - My First Speech In His Divine Presence

Oh! How I Wish I Came To Him Earlier...

How many times does it happen that when we are going through something in life, we wonder why that is happening to us? We are convinced that life would be much better if things would proceed in the manner of our thinking. Hours, days, weeks, months or even years may pass and suddenly, one day, looking back on those very same episodes in life, we are grateful for them because they have made us what we are today.

When it comes to my Swami, my Lord, I feel that I wasted 10 years of my life before having come to know about Him. I wonder how better life would be if only I had known Him earlier and for longer.

Well, in retrospect, when I look at the many things that have happened in life, I am so happy at His perfect timing. For the events that I still do not understand, I have faith that they have happened in the best way possible - only that I am not yet aware of the significance and beauty of the Lord's action.

The Background

Getting on to the time-machine, we move back to 1995. I had wanted to study in Swami's school but was not getting admission at Puttaparthi. Desperate to be in His school, I had got myself admitted at Sri Sathya Sai Vidyapeeth in Calicut, Kerala. I was in grade VIII in 1995 when I was presented with an irresistible offer. Would I like to deliver a speech for *Onam* (the most important festival in Kerala) in Sai Kulwant hall, in Swami's divine presence?

*There is a huge history behind my first speech
in the Divine Presence*

I had just won the Hindi elocution competition then. And so, when I excitedly jumped at the offer, I was told to deliver a speech in Hindi! This was a big challenge. My Hindi was (and is) average at best. The elocution competition victory was simply an ode to my memorizing skills and definitely was not a confirmation of my mastery over Hindi speaking! I decided to use the same method for this speech also. I had two months to prepare. I requested my Hindi teacher to write down my entire speech for me and then began the act of 'mugging', as memorization was called in the school. Weeks of labour and hundreds of rehearsals later, I had become adept at my speech. In fact, if someone woke me up in my sleep and uttered "Aum Sri Sai Ram" - the first line of my speech - I could simply rattle out in the next 10 minutes, my entire speech with the different voice modulations and speed changes!

In order to justify some of the feelings I went through later, I must give a brief background of the atmosphere in my school which was also called Sri Sailam. The school had been performing well academically and so many sought admissions there. However, not everyone who came there was a "Sai devotee". The strict spiritual regimen of morning prayers, food prayers, evening prayers and night prayers, therefore, boiled the angry teenage blood which was present in abundance. This anger and irritation found vent on some of us who were devoted to Swami. Thus, for no fault of His, Swami was blamed as the root for many problems. A constant battle used to be waged between the 'devotees' and the 'non-devotees'.

In fact, even the slightest blemish on our part was instantly attributed to Swami. For instance, if I got involved in a fist fight, the boys would say, "He says he is Baba devotee. Look at him! This is what Baba teaches him!" And that would anger me more. If someone spoke a harsh word about Swami I would speak harsh words about their parents! That would throw them into fits of fury but how was I to make them understand that Swami was as dear as a parent for me? Today, by Swami's grace, I have learnt to deal with critics of all kinds. But back then, I was a novice. I must say that each of those episodes have had a bearing in my changed response to the 'critics'. But that is a different story altogether.

The Prelude To The Story...

Now we get back to the story. I was completely ready for delivering my speech and as the Onam vacations were declared, I rushed to Puttaparthi, with my parents. The school children would be arriving to Puttaparthi in a few days. In the couple of days that I had *darshan* before the school children arrived, an interesting episode occurred.

I wanted to get my speech 'blessed' by Swami. Seated in the *darshan* lines with the script of the speech in hand, I was also reading a book on Lord Krishna called, "The Babe of Brindavan." As Swami came near me in the *darshan* lines, I stretched out both, the book and my speech copy, for Him to bless. He nonchalantly took both in His hand and walked away! I was surprised. What was I to do for that was my only speech copy? (Typing and printing were not common those days – the 1990s).

Swami suddenly stopped. He turned and took the few steps back to me. With a broad smile, He handed back the book. Then He turned and walked away. It was only after the *darshan* session was complete did I realize that Swami had only returned the book and not my speech copy. I went back to my room and wrote down the whole speech again, from my memory.

The Anti-climax

Soon, the contingent from the school arrived. We were given a special place to sit in Sai Kulwant hall for *darshan*. I was eagerly awaiting *Onam* and my chance to speak in His presence. I wanted to ask Swami for one thing that I desperately wanted - admission into His school at Puttaparthi.

The D-day arrived and I was seated on the stage along with another kid who was also supposed to speak. Swami arrived for *darshan* and sat on the dais. He seemed to be waiting for someone or something. Every delayed second made my heart palpitate with anticipation and excitement. I was not rehearsing my speech any more. That I knew too well. I was rehearsing how I would ask Him for admission in His school.

And then, the unforgettable happened. An elderly person was called to deliver a speech. After that, Swami asked for the *Vedam* group to chant in the mikes. Then, He rose to deliver His divine discourse! Our speeches had simply been cancelled! I did not realize it then and was waiting till the end for Swami to call me to deliver my speech. That never happened and Swami received Arati and left! The realization of what had happened came along with tears streaming down my cheek. I was simply shattered.

Later on, a lot of consolation was offered and an explanation too. Apparently, Sri Karunakaran, the former chief minister of

Kerala was to arrive for *Onam*. He cancelled the visit in the last moment by when it was too late for any other programme to be scheduled. So Swami had gone ahead with the discourse. That was no consolation for me who thought, "Why should it be my 10-minute speech that had to suffer because of somebody else's fault?" I was inconsolable.

Matters got worse after we returned to school. The bullies had a new way of taunting and teasing me. "This stupid fool calls Swami his father and mother. If Swami really considered him that way, He would have given him a chance to speak! Hahahaha!" "Look at him! How he fights and quarrels! No wonder he was not given the chance to speak. He simply does not deserve it!" "If your Baba loves you, why did He reject you?"

I had no answers then. I would run away from the taunts into the *bhajan* hall where I would sit and cry in front of His picture. "Swami why did it have to happen this way? If only you had let me speak, nothing of this sort would have happened. I also missed my chance of seeking admission in your school. This is all wrong."

The PUSH Of The Lord...

It is at such times, when we feel that everything is going wrong, that we must remember the PUSH story. This story is a personal favourite and I wish to share it before going ahead.

A man was sleeping at night when suddenly God appeared in his cabin. The Lord told the man that he had some work for him to do and showed him a large rock in front of his door. The Lord explained that the man was to push against the rock with all his might.

The man agreed and did this, day after day. For many years he toiled; his shoulders set squarely against the cold and massive surface of the unmoving rock, pushing with all his might. Each night the man returned to his cabin sore and worn out, feeling that his whole day had been spent in vain.

One day, the devil decided to enter the picture by placing thoughts into the weary mind: "You have been foolishly pushing against that rock for a long time, and it hasn't moved." Satan said, "Why kill yourself over this? Just put in your time, giving just the minimum effort; and that will be good enough. The rock is not going to move anyway." The man was in dilemma and decided to consult the Lord. "Lord," he said, "I have laboured long and hard in your service, putting all my strength to do that which you have asked. Yet, after all this time, I have not even budged that rock by half a millimetre. What is wrong? Why am I failing?"

The Lord responded compassionately, "My friend, when I asked you to serve Me and you accepted, I told you that your task was to push against the rock with all your strength, which you have done. Never once did I mention to you that I expected you to move it. Your task was to simply push."

"And now you come to Me with your strength spent, thinking that you have failed. But, is that really so? Look at yourself. Your arms are strong and muscled, your back sinewy and brown, your hands are callused from constant pressure, and your legs have become massive and hard. Through opposition you have grown much, and your abilities now surpass that which you used to have. You haven't moved the rock. You were never meant to. I wanted you to do this only so that you grow strong. This you have done. Now I, my friend, will move the rock."

Though I was not aware, through all the trials and tribulations of getting teased and being taunted, I was growing. Yet, at that time, all my concentration was on the 'rock' that I felt Swami's heart was which was not being moved at all!

An Attempt At Redemption

I sought another opportunity to speak in His presence so that I could 'redeem' myself in the eyes of my peers and 'friends'. The next year, during *Onam*, our school would have another chance to put up a programme. I hoped to be a part of that somehow. To my utter disappointment, I came to know that the school had a rotation policy of its own. One year the boys would get a chance to do the programme in His presence and the next year would be the turn of the girls. So, I would have to wait for another year at least, to fulfil my hope of speaking in His presence.

Very soon, I found out that I could never be 'redeemed' in the eyes of my 'friends'. Those that loved me and respected me, did not need me to redeem myself. Those that wanted to tease me, would tease and taunt me anyway! Thus, I decided within myself that my endeavour would be only to please Swami. There was no need to have any other objective of speaking in His presence. In order to ensure that I would get that coveted chance the coming year, I began to participate wholeheartedly in all the extra-curricular activities - drama, debate, elocution, singing, recitation. Now when I look back, I know that those were very important years of effort for me and Swami had made me do it with a simple speech cancellation!

The year 1997 was a major one for me because I did get selected to deliver a speech - an English one this time - during the Onam celebrations at Puttaparthi. I was in grade X and thought that this would be the ideal time to request Swami for admission in the school at Prashanti Nilayam for the next year, for grade XI. I prepared with all gusto and awaited, for the second time in my life, for the D-Day when I would deliver the speech.

This time too, I arrived to Puttaparthi a few days before the school. I did not try to get my speech blessed by Swami! This was for two reasons:

1. I felt that He might take it away again.
2. The greater fear was that once He 'accepted' the speech, since He 'knew' the contents already, He might not give me the chance to speak again!

Redemption! Finally!

The *Onam* day arrived. I was sitting in the same place that I sat two years ago. The boys who taunted and teased me were seated in the audience. They had grown and so had the teasing. I had a burning desire to seek from Swami, admission into His school. The teachers had told me to request Swami to come and bless Sri Sailam, the school by a divine visit to Kerala. As Swami completed the *darshan* round and came to the dais, I had déjà-vu! I broke into a cold sweat and imagined what would happen if I did not get a chance to speak again. Swami was seated on His chair when He looked to His right. But this time, instead of beckoning to some elder, He beckoned to me! I got up from my seat and walked slowly towards Swami.

I had seen Swami from close quarters before. But today, when I was the only one around Him on a big stage, I felt so overwhelmed. I went down on my knees near Him and took *padanamaskar* (touching the feet). I rose and then decided to offer my prayer. I looked into His eyes and He looked into mine. I said, "Swami...." In an instant, He was all attention. He prodded me to go on. I don't know what happened at that instant. In a flash, I recollected all that I had gone through to get this opportunity. And was I going to waste it by asking for something as less as a high school admission?

I looked at Him and said, "Swami, please keep me with you throughout my life..." He asked me to repeat my words. "Swami, please keep me with you throughout my life." I said firmly. He seemed so happy with my answer. He patted me lovingly on the head and nodded as if to say yes. Then, He told me to go and speak.

Part of me was telling me that I had done the best thing. Another part was telling me that I should have asked for admission into school. I thought I would ask about it after my speech. The speech went off like a breeze. There were two applauses - I don't remember for what. I was simply overwhelmed. As I concluded and walked to Him, I turned and saw all my classmates and schoolmates cheering for me. When the Lord blesses you, the world simply comes to your side! I was filled with such love and magnanimity. I prayed for all my friends as I walked to Swami. And in that happy mood, instead of asking for admission, I said, "Swami, please come to Sri Sailam." Swami blessed me with a pat and a smile but did not reply to me. I took *namaskar* and returned to my place.

There was Swami's discourse after that. I did not hear a thing. I was so lost in joy. I had no regret about not asking for admission. I was simply glad that I had sought the right thing and I thanked Swami for it!

The realisation of a dream and much more...

To complete this story, I must say what happened three days later. Swami said that He would bless all the students from the Kerala school for He was very happy with us. He began to move amidst us, collecting letters and blessing all. I thought that this was when I would seek my admission. As Swami came in front of me, I rose on my knees. At the same time, He placed His hand on my head and pushed me down. It was as if He did not want me to seek anything lesser than the highest - and that I had already sought. What happened next is enshrined in my heart...

Swami is about 5 meters away from me when He suddenly stops and asks, "You spoke yesterday didn't you?" I nod. Then as He moves ahead, He turns back and asks,

"What are you studying?"
"Swami class X"
"Class XI....after class XII what?" (in Tamil)
"Swami whatever you say."
"No...Medical or Engineering - which do you like?"
"Swami medical."
"Medical! Study Biosciences here and get good marks."

I got my admission next year. I got something far greater too - the chance to be with Him throughout life.

The Masterplan

Today, when I look back at that episode, I realize the Love of Swami. If He had given me the chance to speak two years before, I would have sought admission in His school from Him. He wanted me to ask for the highest, Himself, and He was ready to wait for me to grow to that stage. He 'delayed' the chance so that I could benefit the most from it. As I think of it, my heart oozes in love and gratitude to Him.

What I learned that day is so beautifully put by Swami in the thought for the day that I received on 4th of April 2012 by email from Sai Inspires.

Do not waste your life in making arrangements,
For they have already been made.
Use that time wisely instead to do prayers,
And seeking Me in all, in every living form.

Only have faith in My arrangements,
And know that I am present
At all times everywhere.
All you have to do is to ask for My help.
I require no time to travel.
My presence is certain anywhere,
Where I am sincerely thought of.
In fact, your thought of Me, and My presence
Are instantaneous.

Chapter Four

Sai Student

Being a student of the Sathya Sai Institute of Higher Learning, I have always called myself a Sai student. Based on that experience, I have come to develop some of my own expectations of a Sai Student. I also know to some measure what the society expects of a Sai Student. But what does Swami expect of a Sai Student? Who is a Sai Student? This is probably something that the reader should know before I share my experiences as His student.

Once, Swami had told a student, "Remember, just because you are a student of the Institute does not automatically imply that you are a Sai Student!"

And here is what I learnt on what Swami's views are on what His student is. This was shared to me by a Sai brother who has been blessed by His grace to travel with Him to Kodaikanal.

I present what he narrated:

It was a pleasant morning in Kodaikanal in 2006. We all sang bhajans as Swami went around giving *darshan* and filling devotees seated there with bliss. After the bhajans we all rushed to the drawing room for the "pre-lunch" session of interaction with Swami. Swami was visibly very upset with something! He was not talking to anyone.

And the few words He spoke were shocking, " I want to leave this body".

The Most Touching And Startling Revelation...

Every one of us was taken aback and was crying. Warden Sir (Sri Narasimhamoorthy) asked Swami, "Swami, please tell us what is it that is bothering you so much? What mistake have we committed that it is paining you so much? What is it that made you utter these words? **Swami we are ready to give our lives for you if needed.**"

Swami did not say a word. He kept silent. That day, we all were sent for shopping. But none of us had any interest in shopping. Still, since they were the instructions that were conveyed to us by the elders, we obeyed them. Generally, Swami used to ask all the boys as to what they bought and that, in itself, would be a lovely interactive session. But that day the entire atmosphere was different, we also strictly decided not to bring any of our purchases downstairs.

Even during the snacks time Swami did not speak anything. We all went for *bhajans* (devotional singing) in the evening. During the *bhajans* Swami suddenly asked for the mikes to be brought. The first few sentences He spoke were these and they remain etched in my memory -

"**Who are you to give up your lives?** I do not want you to die! What I want you all to do is to LIVE THE WAY I WANT YOU TO LIVE. From the time I get up in the morning till the time I go to bed I think constantly about you only. When you are with Me you are all very sweet and behave very well. But the moment you leave my physical presence, you get into the bad ways.

It is like the pot of water which is kept in the water. It is full only as long as it is immersed in the water. But the moment it is taken out of the water, the water in the pot starts evaporating. I don't have any desire. **Nenu Nishkamudanu** - I am the one without desire.

My only worry is about you all. I want you to be good and be ideals to be emulated. From the morning, I have not been talking and have seemingly been upset. Some of the boys around me asked the reason and some even said that they are ready to give up their lives for me. Whose life is it that you want to give it up? Do not die for me, live for me."

All of us were in tears and Swami too was shedding tears.

"Merely studying in Sathya Sai University
does not make you a Sai student."

A True Sai Student

Devotion lies not in dying for God, but living for God - in the spirit of Love and Service. I understood the difference between a Sathya Sai University Student and a Sai Student. Only a few get a chance to be the former; only a few take the chance to be the latter! Being a student of the University alone does not make one a Sai Student. A Sai Student is one who is a true student of Sai's teachings!

If only all of us can truly become His students...

Chapter Five

My First Memorable Interaction With Sathya Sai As His Student

The Inexplicable Silence...

I always felt that when I became a devotee of Sri Sathya Sai Baba, He got me free and quick! Allow me to explain through a little detour. I first saw Swami through photographs when I was just about 7 years old. I used to wonder who this person with curly hair was. My father used to keep photos of Swami at home because he had been to Swami when he was about 12 years old. His experiences are the subject of some other article(s). Anyway, the highlight of his arrival to Swami was his thread ceremony. The sacred thread ceremony (called *Upanayanam*) is important for every *Brahmin* in India. Swami had performed this ceremony for my father and had whispered the holy *Gayatri mantra* (a powerful invocation with great spiritual benefits) into his ears. And this was while seating him on His own lap. Since then, my father had a string of experiences that bound him inseparably with Swami.

But strangely, after marriage, he had become very silent about Swami. Though marriage is known to silence men, it did not hold true in that sense for father. My mother, in no way had a role in 'suppressing' Swami in any manner. In fact, she was always keen to know about Swami. Today, in retrospect, I feel that it was only His will that my father kept silent about Him after his marriage. None can come to Swami without His will!

My Introduction To My Lord - Instantaneous And Firm

That was, till I began to ask him about Swami. I kept pointing to Swami's picture in our home and asked my father who that person was. My father had first replied to me that He was the one who had performed his thread ceremony. I thus assumed that Swami was a priest of some sort who initiated people into chants. But then, I got another doubt that I guess, irked my father. I asked,

"Father, why keep a picture of only that priest who performed your thread ceremony? What about the priest who performed your marriage or my naming ceremony for that matter?"

Exasperated and desperate, my father told me,

"You want to know who He is? He is God. Worship Him and He will take care of you in every way."

At that instant, I believed in Sathya Sai and placed my faith in Him. I also seemed to develop some kind of unquenchable attraction and love for Him. It was as simple as that.

Now you will understand what I mean by saying that Swami got me free and quick. When I read accounts and narratives of devotees, I came to know of wondrous miracles that brought them to Swami and convinced them of His Divinity. I felt that by accepting Him straight, I had missed the opportunity to throw a challenge at Him and get an 'experience' for myself! The debate between faith and experience - as to which begets which - is a raging one and I got an answer for that debate much later in my life. Anyway, I was happy because implicit faith has its own advantages.

My Resolve On Joining God's School...

When I joined the Sathya Sai Higher Secondary School in 1998, my mother told me, "From now on, Swami is your mother, your father, friend and God. Share everything with Him and He will take care." Armed with that advice, I entered the hostel. When I first arrived to the hostel, my concept was that it would be the perfect *gurukula* (ancient Indian hermitage where the teachers would stay with students. The students would be all treated as equal irrespective of the families and backgrounds they came from).

It is not that it wasn't, but it did not match exactly my concept of the *gurukula*. The teachers definitely spoke a lot about Swami and values were valued. I still remember my physics teacher, Sairam Sir, asking us in the first class that he took, as to what were our aims to study in this hallowed place.

The answers that arose that time made me feel as if I was seated in an assembly of sages! One said, "I want to serve the society till the last breath." Another said, "Like Vivekananda, I too would like to realize my true self!"

It was my turn to answer. The first impression is the best one they say. I wanted to speak something that would make everyone sit up and listen with awe and respect. And so I got up and said, "I want to be with Swami."

It did not create the sensation that I had desired as there was nothing brilliant in that answer, but I could think of nothing else! And maybe that is the thing about the Truth. It falls out so easily from the heart and the mouth that it actually requires an effort to speak a lie. And that must be why our ancients always advised us to speak the Truth!

A *gurukula* is special because of the interaction between the Guru and the students. Swami was undoubtedly the Guru here and I longed for interactions with Him. I wondered as to how I would achieve it. It was on a jogging trip to the Hanuman statue on top of the Vidyagiri hill that I discovered the answer. (At least I thought at that time that I did!) As we jogged, my senior from the grade XII pointed to a tall and lanky student and said,

"You know that Prashant. He is a form boy." I wondered what that meant and also pondered whether there was anything like "formless" boys? "He is not formless like us," he completed, even as I was thinking about it! I knew of 'deformed' boys and maybe even 'reformed' ones but these two categories just mentioned were entirely new. My thoughts must have played clearly on my face for the senior said in a lowered voice,

"Swami likes him a lot and speaks to him a lot. He is close to Swami." It was then that I understood that the term "form" had been borrowed from the sport of Cricket! A batsman in form is always admired. And when he performs below par, he is "out of form." So I assumed that "formless" were those who had never made it 'big' anytime! Now my mind also began to jog with my body and soon was sprinting furiously. Not exactly the person to believe completely in destiny and give up freewill, I thought, "Well. There must be some reason why he is so dear to Swami. I will find out and soon will get into 'form'." I remember sitting at my study desk in the night writing in my diary,

"Today I have made a decision. I will become a form boy of Swami."

My 'Love Letter' To Him...

Every night in the hostel, we were given special sheets of paper on which we could write the name of any form of the Lord we loved. This was part of the *Sadhana* that students could take part in. While different students wrote either, "Jai Sri Krishna" or "Aum Sri Sai Ram" or any other name as per their choice, I wrote, "I love you Swami."

Every night, I wrote that hundreds of times. We were told that all our "*Sadhana* sheets" could be submitted and they would be offered to Swami. The sheets would then be used to pack the holy *vibhuti* prasadam. I felt shy of submitting my writings and so, I placed the sheet in my own altar in my cupboard.

Suddenly a thought struck me,

"All the *Sadhana* of the other students is being offered to Swami. But my sheet is lying in my cupboard. I should offer it to Swami myself."

My plan was to offer the sheet on which I had professed my love for Him like a letter. Satisfying myself thus, I took the letter one evening for *darshan*. I felt that if the intensity of my love was true, Swami should accept my 'letter' on the same evening. I was seated in the centre of a group of students. I wondered as to how Swami would ever be able to take my letter as I was a minimum of six people away from Him from all sides of the group. And sure enough, as I thought, the *Darshan* session was over and the letter still remained with me. Swami took a group of devotees for interview. About half an hour later, He came out. He came walking till where we were seated and I was just watching curiously.

Then, all of a sudden, Swami told two students to part and make way. Just like the sea giving way to Moses, the students made a path for Swami to wade amidst us. In the new path that was formed, I was in the second line and so would be within Swami's 'reach'. Immediately, my ego took over. I felt like some great devotee of the Lord who had pulled the Lord to Himself, by the sheer power of his devotion. My chest puffed up and I awaited Him. As He came near, I extended my 'letter' and He accepted it! I bent my head down to look at His feet when a sheet of paper fell by my side. I was surprised to see that it was the letter I had given Him. I quickly picked it and looked upwards to give it back to Him. But, Swami had walked away by then! I was shocked and devastated. My bloated ego fizzled out and I reprimanded myself, "You thought you were a great devotee and see what happened! Remember that it is always God's grace..."

However, tears dropped from my eyes. I was sad. In an instant, I had travelled from heights of joy and pride, to depths of sorrow and feeling inferior. How I wish I knew how to tread the amazing middle path!

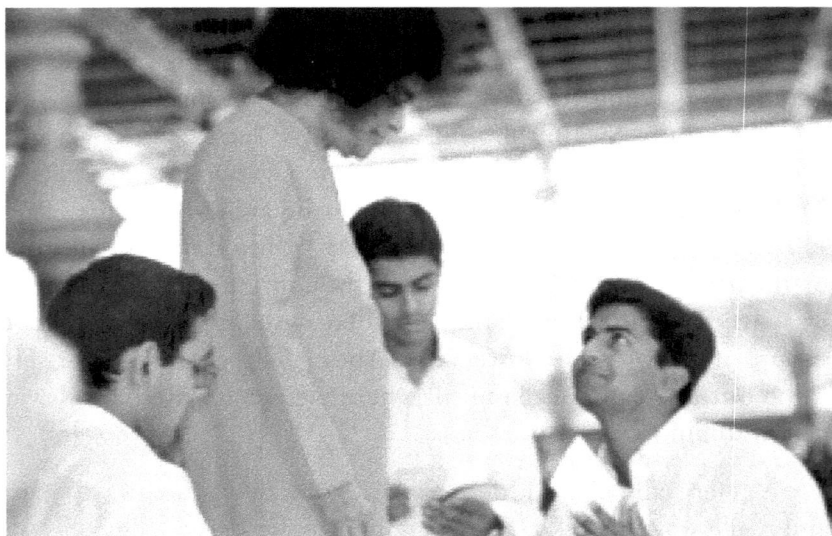

I learned that Swami and not my ego
should be my focus always.

The Love Of My Life...

Swami moved a little ahead and began to wave His palm. He had materialized *vibhuti* (sacred ash) for some fortunate devotee. The practice those days was that when Swami created *vibhuti* for anyone, any student who had a clean white kerchief could offer the same to Swami to wipe His hands on. Since I had a handkerchief with me, I rushed to Swami. He did not even look at me. Looking at the devotees, He took the kerchief and wiped His right hand. He threw back the kerchief at me. As I held it, He suddenly turned and patted me on my shoulder.

I was taken aback. I looked up at Him and He had a smile on His face. He seemed to be pointing at my pocket and when I saw there, I realised that He wanted my letter! Oh! Was I thrilled. I fished the letter out of my pocket and He accepted it. He placed it safely in His hands and then walked on. I returned to my place.

Again, I had tears in my eyes. Only this time, they were tears of joy! The timing, the situation, the whole episode - everything seemed to have built up to this crescendo. I knew that I had found the love of my life.

Chapter Six

The Day Swami Blessed Me By Telling Me To Join The Mental Hospital...

Coincidence Or A Miracle?

There seems to be a fine line between coincidental and miraculous for the 'scientific' critic as well as the religious zealot. And both use this line variably, as per convenience, to see the miraculous as coincidental or the coincidental as miraculous. The truth, however, is that no such line exists! Coincidences are miracles where God simply chooses to be anonymous. Before I dive and delve into one such powerful yet funny 'coincidental' experience in my life, I must say that there are parts to this experience which I understood much later.

It was during my student days in Sri Sathya Sai Higher Secondary School that this episode occurred. Bubbling with energy and enthusiasm, I used to strive at every opportunity to get Swami to talk to me, touch me or look at me. I felt that if a day passed without Swami doing any of the above, it would be a waste of a valuable day. Praying was one thing, but jumping around and trying hard to come into His line of sight was another! I indulged whole-heartedly and completely in both.

One thing that is true with Swami is that His plans and our plans do not always match! Our's plans are based on very limited knowledge and infinite selfishness! His plans are part of the Master Plan - based on complete knowledge and infinite selflessness. And so, as the devotee would have certainly discovered in life, one's plan and God's plan seem to go out of sync on many occasions. Thus, though I thought that Swami should speak or interact with me in some manner on a daily basis, it rarely happened so. Days would pass when He would not even look at me!

A pleasant surprise

I was pleasantly shocked when He spoke to me on the 2nd of January, 2000. It was a 'normal' Sunday. (The word normal is in quotes because in reality, no day with the divine can be considered normal. Every day is special if we spend it seeing, hearing, talking about and thinking of the divine). Sunday was the day when we would have two *darshan* sessions since there were no classes in the morning. I was seated along the lines of the school students. When Swami came for *darshan*, gently gliding on the hem of His robe, I stretched out a letter that I had written to Him. In the letter, I had sought Him to be in my life forever. Swami looked at me and then said, *"Mental hospital ko join karna better."* (It is better if you go and get admitted in a mental hospital.) And then He walked on.

During those days, wherever I was (on the right side in the photo), He saw me and told me to join the Mental Hospital.

I rejoiced! There is the story of a villager's son who came running and told his father that the king had spoken to him. The father heard him out and jubilantly summoned the whole village to announce the glad tidings. It turned out that the lad had been lazing in the middle of the road. The king who was moving on his chariot shouted out, "Oh! You lazy fool! Get out of this highway and do something useful in life." Despite the content of what the king said, the fact that he spoke was enough to thrill the lad.

My condition was something similar. I was so thrilled that Swami spoke to me. The evening *darshan* turned out to be memorable too.As Swami came gliding past during *darshan*, I stretched out my hand with the letter. Swami stopped, turned and looked at me. He smiled and told the people around me,"This boy has come from mental hospital. He must be sent back there." And so, it continued for a couple more times in the next two days. Swami would look at me and make references to the mental hospital. As long as nobody took it literally and made efforts to get me enrolled into one, I was happy at these interactions. Swami was SPEAKING WITH ME!

Then, one day, suddenly, Swami seemed to forget about my need to get enrolled in a mental hospital. It went back to Him not 'recognising' me and I went back to my jumpy self, making all efforts to attract His attention!

The Sports and Cultural Meet of the Sri Sathya Sai Institutions took place. The *Sankranti* festival along with prize distribution was completed. It was now time for the preparatory exams before the much feared Board Examinations, (held by the Central Board of Secondary Education at an All-India level), that every 12th grade student has to pass through. The schedule for the preparatory exams had been put up and we were all busy studying.

The final part of the 'mental hospital' episode took place in this situation. It was the day before the biology exam. I was sitting on the lawns in front of the hostel and studying when I noticed some boys playing with the garden hose pipe. They were spraying and squirting water on each other in a playful manner. I got tempted to join them and gladly yielded to my temptation too!

After about 15 minutes, I realised that I had a lot to study and so, though wet, returned to my books. But my determination to study lasted only about 10 minutes after which I went again to play with the water pipe. Once again, my conscience pricked me and I returned to study. This to and fro between studies and water-sports went on for a while after which I felt frustrated. I took a step that I felt would prevent me from any further distraction. I closed my eyes and told Swami, "Swami, I will read two chapters before I have food. If I do not do so, I shall not have my lunch."

That promise, I thought, would stop me from indulging in the water-war that was happening on the lawns. It did not! I was soon back to spraying water when I heard the lunch gong. I was definitely hungry and there was no time to read two chapters before lunch. The hostel is strict about timings and naturally so. (One cannot deal with 300 students if there is no strict adherence to discipline and timings). In case I went 10-15 minutes late for lunch, I was sure to be told that I had arrived too early for dinner!Caught in that predicament, my mind impishly schemed a plan. "I promised Swami that I would 'read' two chapters and not 'study' two chapters; that I can accomplish in fifteen minutes!" Consoling myself thus, I simply read through the two chapters at lightning speed. Having finished doing that, I smiled to myself and went for lunch.

The evening *darshan* saw me seated in the first row along the path through which Swami would walk. Seated next to me was a staff member of the Central Trust. As Swami came gliding through the path, he told this senior brother next to me, "Take this fellow to the mental hospital and get him admitted there." I was happy that the good old days had come back.

Swami moved on. Taking a few steps, He suddenly stopped, turned back and delivered an unforgettable line, "And when you admit him there, do not give him food to eat!"

I had goose bumps! I was so thrilled and lost in awe at the same time. Oh my God! My promise! And here is the punch. The staff member to whom Swami spoke was also smiling. What Swami said was special for him too. This was because, Swami had used the Telugu term '*Annam*' to refer to food and his name happened to be Annam!

Talk about Swami's 'omnifelicity' where he can make multiple people feel special with a single act of His! We should add it to His standard qualities of omnipresence, omnipotence and omniscience. Was that a coincidence? I beg to differ. Though it is said that coincidences are miracles where God chooses to remain anonymous, here was a case where He had not remained so.

It was much later that I came across what Swami says, "Of all the madnesses that afflict man, God-madness is the least harmful and the most beneficial." The complete statement of Swami is on the Radiosai page.

Some people talk caustically to Sai devotees saying: "You have gone crazy over Sai Baba". This craziness is sublime madness. There are all kinds of lunatics in the mental hospital, many of whom pose difficult problems for the doctors. If some God-mad devotee sits in a corner chanting God's name, what a relief he would be to the doctors! If you develop this kind of sublime madness, you will be supremely fortunate indeed! Everyone should be crazy about God. Only then they will get rid of the mad craving for wealth and the things of the world.

I wished that Swami's statements of me joining the mental hospital came true and I was admitted there with God-madness.

Chapter 7

The Handkerchief Mischief Of My Sweet Lord

If we take any aspect of Swami's physical life, we see that it has changed and evolved according to the time, place, person and situation. The way He grants *darshan*, for instance, has changed from walking among a few dozen people in a small hall to walking in a disciplined gathering of thousands (with musical accompaniment) to personal appearances at the homes of the devotees themselves currently! And in between this spectrum of three distinct points that I have mentioned are many intermediate stages. Each of these stages have their own speciality.

During the late 90's and early years of the new millennium, Swami used to bless the students with one special kind of chance – the handkerchief chance. Before I proceed to narrate three interesting stories, let me detail on this kerchief chance.

Unlike the years before and after, 1997-2001 saw Swami walk alone during *darshan* without anyone following Him. So, He would collect and carry all the letters which devotees offered on His own. Thus, when He materialised *vibhuti* for any devotee, any student in possession of a handkerchief could run up to Him and offer the same for Him to wipe His hands. And I was one among the many students who decided to build a relationship with Him through this 'kerchief chance'! In fact, my first, memorable interaction with Him was also through this kerchief chance.

Episode 1 – Harmless And Joy-giving Mischief

It was one hot afternoon in the holy hamlet and all of us students were assembled in the Sai Kulwant hall by 3:15 pm for *darshan*. I got a chance to be seated in the first line and since I had a handkerchief in my pocket, I feverishly hoped that Swami would create *vibhuti* for some devotee who was seated near me. I could see another boy who was also cuddling a handkerchief in his pocket. If Swami created *vibhuti* at little distance away from me, then the 'kerchief chance' would fall in that other boy's 'territory'! And so, I was hoping that it would happen close to me! I scanned out the faces of devotees with the hope of being able to locate one who might be in 'distress' and thus deserve the materialised *vibhuti*. Today I realize that all these efforts are so foolish but those were my ways then. And almost every other kerchief-chance-seeking-lad had similar ways.

Darshan began. The gentle music floated through the air and the Lord floated into the hall. He seemed to glide so beautifully. One would find it hard to believe that He was actually walking – the full-sized robe made it seem like He was skimming over the land surface. When He was just a few feet away from me, He materialised *vibhuti* for a devotee. It was in my 'territory'! I was overjoyed! I rushed to Him with the kerchief.

He took the kerchief from me and wiped His hands. And then, instead of throwing back the kerchief to me, He threw it down. It fell down straight on His lotus feet. I thought that I would wait till He moved ahead and then pick up the kerchief before returning to my place. And then, the unexpected happened! As Swami walked ahead, I saw that there was no kerchief on the ground! I wondered as to what had happened? Had some devotee taken the kerchief as a token of Swami's blessings and grace? It was very much possible – in the bygone days, people used to collect the sand on which He walked as a treasure! I began to scout the devotees quickly to see who had taken away 'my' blessed kerchief. Even as I searched desperately for about 9-10 seconds, I saw smiles blossom on the faces of many devotees.

I looked up and saw Swami at a distance. He was about 10 feet from me. He turned around, smiled and gently shook His foot.

And then, as He walked on, I saw the kerchief neatly deposited on the floor. The mischievous Swami had held the kerchief with His foot and had carried it away! Now, a smile blossomed on my face too. I walked the ten feet, picked up the kerchief and returned to my place.

The beauty of His mischief is that it never hurts anyone – it makes everyone around happy. How wonderful if all our mischief too can be that positive and beautiful?

Whenever Swami materialised Vibhuthi for a devotee, any
student could offer a handkerchief to Him for wiping His hands.

Episode 2 - Love My Uncertainty

On another occasion, the 'kerchief-chance' competition really had heated up. It was a session when two of us with handkerchiefs were sitting side-by-side. Just like any devotee who wished to give a letter could get a letter, any student who wished could get a kerchief. There were no restrictions. (In fact, many devotees too would get handkerchiefs with the hope that they would be able to beat the student and offer the same to Swami!) Thus, I knew, if Swami created *vibhuti* I would have to be really quick to outrun my 'competitor'.

That is the beauty of being with Swami. Competition gets created for who can get first to the Lord - a far better alternative to the rat races that exist for money, position and fame.

Swami came for *darshan*. As He came near where we were seated, He began to talk quite a lot with a devotee. Now, this meant that there was a high chance of that devotee getting *vibhuti*. My muscles tensed and I saw my 'competitor' tense his muscles too. He was sitting by my side and I could feel his muscles tensing! "I have to be real quick if I have to get this chance", I thought.

And then, Swami slightly moved and began to encircle His palm. Ah! That is a sign that He is materialising *vibhuti*. Even before He could create the same, I got up and rushed to Him with the handkerchief. I had beaten my competitor who was still sitting. With jubilation at this victory and the anticipation of the 'kerchief-chance' with Swami, I went to Him.

What an anti-climax it was!

Swami did indeed wave His palm. But instead of the fragrant, grey ash, out came an emerald-studded ring. Even as He placed the ring on the devotee's finger, He seemed to look at me questioningly. It was as if He was asking me, "Why did you come running here?"

A strict disciplinarian that He is, I got so scared. I returned back to my place at double the speed at which I went to Swami. Everyone there were smiling and laughing. It was with great relief that I saw my fear turn into a joke and I too joined in the laughter.

"Love my uncertainty", Swami says. We love it only when we get unexpected bounties, but can we love it even when things seem to go wrong?

Episode 3 - God Has A Plan For Me And That Is All I Need To Know

This time, Swami created *vibhuti* for a student. Three of us students rushed to Him with a handkerchief. Each one of us had started off at the same time and though each one saw the others, nobody wanted to give up. And so, all three of us kneeled before Him with our respective handkerchiefs. Now, it looked real funny! We were wondering as to what He would do. I secretly hoped that He would simply wipe His hands on all the three handkerchiefs being offered. In that way, everyone would be happy. But what Swami told was totally the opposite. He told all of us to put the kerchiefs back in our pockets! When I was hoping He would bless all the three of us, He seemed to have decided to bless none of us!

Even as we put the kerchiefs into our pockets, came the unexpected masterstroke.

Swami told each one of us to stretch out our hands and gave us also the same *vibhuti* which He had materialised! We were pleasantly shocked. Presently, a fourth student came to Swami with a handkerchief and Swami wiped His hands on that! The fourth guy was also thrilled at this unexpected bounty.

God's plans for us are always way better than our plans for ourselves. If only we can hold on for that extra bit longer, we will enjoy His love and grace in greater measure!

Chapter Eight

"Satyameva Jayate" - Truth Alone Triumphs

The Discipline And Practice Of 'Mandir Lines'

A very interesting episode occurred during my school days. Today, when I look back at it in retrospect, I see that it shows the immaturity of a child's thinking and the 'maturity' of Swami's love! This happened when I was in 11th grade (1998) when I had taken the combination BPC (Bio Science, Physics and Chemistry) for my studies.

Before I narrate that episode, let me tell you about the mandir lines. Every day, we would go to the *mandir* (for Baba's *darshan*) from the hostel in ordered lines. And to ensure that everyone had equal chances of getting physically close to Swami, each day different classes would go first. For instance, if the first day, the order of the lines would be classes VIII, IX , X, XI and XII, the next day the order would be IX, X, XI, XII, VIII and so on, in a cycle. Sundays were special because we would go even for the morning *darshan* as it was a holiday. The Sundays had a special rotation system of its own with the cycle changing every week! And this whole thing would be manned by the teachers.

That was fine as far as equality of classes was concerned. But, what about the order of students within a class? There was an unwritten rule (made by the boys, of the boys and for the boys) - anyone who could get ready with a wash, shave and a *vibhuti* dot on the forehead could rush down to the assembling point after (and only after) the bell for forming lines had been rung. The order of the boys in different rows would then get determined as 1.1, 1.2, 1.3, 2.1, 2.2, 2.3 and so on. If anyone was not neatly shaved and washed or missed the *vibhuti* dot, he would be disqualified and his position confiscated by the next boy in the order. At times, this would force us to go to classes after a complete wash up. This was especially true for the post-lunch sessions on the days when our class would be first.

Giving letters and offering the kerchief were my chief occupations as a student in Higher Secondary School.

Fiasco At The Chemistry Lab

On this particular day, we were having our Chemistry lab sessions. As a class we had disappointed the teacher concerned and he was in an irritable mood. It was also the day when our class would be first in the lines and there was a nervous energy all around. We were all the students of the Science section. There were students of the Commerce section too from our class and so our silent hope was that our class would be let out earlier than theirs. (You see, there were so many levels of competition to be overcome to get first into the lines!)

With ten minutes to go, all of us began to automatically wash the glassware and started winding up for the day. It was a tough task and in the hurry to finish fast, a few beakers cracked and broke. Needless to say, this irritated the teacher even more. None of us have ever paid any laboratory fees and all the chemicals and glassware are provided to us with love by Swami. (And that is because Swami believes that education is the right of every child and not a privilege!) While other labs have breakage charges, there are none in our labs. So, naturally, the least that is expected of us is to maintain these gifts of love with care.

I too was washing away furiously in a hurry, taking care that no glassware breaks. Finally, within a minute of the final bell, all the glassware had been washed and arranged in the shelves. My legs were waiting with pent up energy for the rush to capture a front spot in the lines. As fate would have it, the teacher began to inspect the washed glassware and he located one beaker that had remnants of the organic chemicals that had been used. He immediately picked it up and asked "Whose beaker is this?"

I realised that it was mine. And I was caught between the horns of a dilemma. Immediately the little white angel on my right and the little red devil on my left began their traditional conversation! "Just keep quiet. There is no way he will find out it is your beaker.

He will get frustrated and let go." "No! That is not right. You know that it is yours and you should own up. Moreover, instead of letting go, he may punish the whole class." "You raise your hand now and your chance to be front in the lines is gone! The chance to get physically near to Swami is too great to be left for the sake of a chemical drop on a beaker!" "You know that the problem is not as skewed as the devil is putting it. Remember that more than the nearness, the dearness to Swami matters.By following the truth, you will please Him." "*Satyameva Jayate* (Truth alone triumphs) is a motto for the aeons gone by. It is not relevant now." "Truth is for ever and it always triumphs. You speak the truth and you will be rewarded. That is for sure."

"Tell me! Whose beaker is this?", the voice thundered. I immediately raised my hand and said, "I am sorry Sir! That is mine." The teacher's eyes immediately seemed to calm down.

He said, "All can leave now." Even as I prepared for the sprint, he said, "Aravind. Stay back."

I was punished. I was given a load of glassware to wash and then alone could I leave for the *mandir*. I was immediately fraught with disappointment and sadness. It then erupted as anger within me. "I thought that speaking the truth will save me. It only put me in deeper problem. Forget the front lines, I doubt whether I will even be in time for *darshan*!" As I angrily continued the washing, I failed to notice that the teacher had punished himself too - by not going to the *mandir* till I was done. I was too busy with my own 'misfortune' to think about him. My mind continued to speak "This *Satyameva Jayate* really seems to be relevant only for the past. I don't care how, but if it is relevant even in the modern times, then Swami, I want you to bless me today. I want you to accept a handkerchief from me and smile at me. I don't know how you will do it but you must do it if you want me to have faith in the truth."

I threw this as a challenge at Him. I felt slightly happy within because I was in a win-win situation. At a time when I was sure to be late for *darshan*, if Swami were to give me that chance of offering a handkerchief to Him, my day would be so special. In case that did not happen, I would have no problem lying myself out of future situations! (There! This is what I referred to as the immaturity of the child.)

A Lesson Well-learned

Finishing my punishment, I informed the teacher who was still waiting patiently for me. He too seemed sad. I felt that he deserved to miss *darshan* for he had made me miss my share of it. (Later, I found out that he was sad because he felt responsible for me missing *darshan* and he was praying to Swami to wait till I arrived! Wow! The teachers here are some magical creatures of love!)

I went to the *mandir* and there was no music on. I was sure that *darshan* had been complete. I was shocked to find out that for some reason, Swami had not yet arrived for *darshan*! (This was very rare. Swami was always on time!) And as I walked in to the students' area, I saw one empty space right in the first line. How could anyone have missed it? I asked the boy seated there whether that space was reserved for someone and he replied in a negative. Once again, the immature thinking set in. "Swami wants to make it easy for Himself to prove to you the importance of Truth. If I sit here, He will create *vibhuti* for some devotee and take the handkerchief from me. I shall not make it that easy for Him!"

Thinking thus, I gave up that space and went to sit in the portico outside the interview room. This was a region that was manned by two boys assisting Swami's and in case He created *vibhuti* here, they would offer the kerchief to Him. I wanted concrete proof of His response and as I did this, I could see the little red devil snickering at the little white angel. I felt a little guilty too, but I went ahead with my plan.

What happened next, completely bowled me over. I sat in the portico and the *darshan* music began. Swami arrived and completed

His *darshan* rounds. He came to the portico and began to speak to some devotee.-At the end of the two-minute interaction, He began to swirl His palm to create *vibhuti*. He gifted the *vibhuti* to the devotee. I was a good 3 meters away from Him. But, out of sheer instinct, I had tugged the kerchief out of my pocket. However, I stayed put in my place and one of the two assistants went to Swami with a handkerchief.

Swami just looked away from him into my eyes. He smiled and stretched out His hand, seeking the kerchief in my hand. Like a robot, I got up from my place and went to Him. I gave the handkerchief to Him. He wiped His hand, smiled at me and threw the kerchief back to me. I returned to my place in a daze.

The mesmerising smile He gave me that day is something unforgettable

Even as I sat, my senior beside me nudged me and said, "You are a 'form' boy! He specially wanted you. Did you have some sort of a prayer-deal with Him?"

What could I say? I realized that a win-win situation for me was also a win-win situation for Him. His love is such that He wins if I win. One thing is for sure - I know that Truth Always Triumphs.

Chapter Nine

The Middle Path - The Golden Mean - As Taught To Me By My Swami

The Middle Path

There is something beautiful and charming about the 'middle path'. In any situation which demands taking a decision based on some unknowns, we choose the 'average' route or the 'middle path'. Say someone asks you, "Are you ever-steady in your faith in God?" Any person wanting to answer this in complete honesty would usually answer, "I guess so", "Maybe, it is steady" OR "I guess not", "I think I falter sometimes".

Choosing a midway answer is so much easier than a "black & white" answer like "Yes" or "No".

Forget about the jest, the profundity of the middle path was wonderfully discovered by Lord Buddha. He described it as the easiest and surest pathway to liberation; a path that is characterised by moderation between the extremes of sensual indulgence and self-mortification. Today, that is famous as the 'Golden Mean'.

Centuries ago, Lord Krishna too emphasised on this 'middle path' while conferring the Bhagwad Gita to Arjuna. (He did not use that term though!) He used the term, *"Sthitapragnya"* or one of equipoise. Krishna explained to Arjuna that a *Sthitapragnya* has an even mind, which is neither elated by joy nor dejected by sorrow. The *Sthitapragnya* dwells always in the Spirit without giving way to grief, lust, fear and delusion. His vision beholds the Spirit everywhere. Krishna pointed out that Arjuna would be able to realise His true nature (or gain liberation) only when he becomes a *Sthitapragnya*.

In this regard, Swami says that while Self-Confidence is necessary, pride and show are bad. Similarly, while humility is necessary, self-condemnation and degrading oneself are bad.

Self-Confidence and Humility are not opposites but an inseparable pair - the middle path. And my experience with Bhagawan Baba was based on this. This brief introduction was necessary to enjoy the chiselling that Swami performed to mould a more complete personality of me.

The Decision To Stay In The Hostel During Vacations

When I finally got a chance to be a student in the Sri Sathya Sai Higher Secondary School, I was very thrilled and excited. Here was my chance to be and stay with Swami, studying in a school that He had started! In the first few weeks itself, I got the chance to experience His omnipresence and love. Those experiences made me thirst more and more for His physical proximity and for chances to interact with Him. I made a plan which I felt was a fool proof way of winning His grace. Swami has always emphasised the Vedic dictum, *"Na Karmana Na Prajaya Dhanena Tyagenaike Amritatwa Manashuhu."* This means, "Neither action, nor progeny nor wealth will confer immortality. Only sacrifice confers immortality."

People have often made sacrifices to please God - fasting, abstaining from indulgence in desires, giving up things etc. (In fact, Swami has pointed out that instead of sacrificing 'animal qualities' for God, people change it conveniently and carry out animal sacrifice which is a terrible sin!) I too decided to sacrifice something very dear to me to please my God - Swami! I thought that when the winter vacation arrived (20th - 31st October, 1998), I would stay back and not go home. I would sacrifice my vacation as an offering for Him. I knew in a corner of my heart that Swami would be pleased and would respond to my 'sacrifice'. Before I move on, I must make a point about 'sacrifice' here. When one decides to sacrifice, it means one is giving up something that one loves for the sake of something that one loves greater! Swami often jokes about a situation where a person goes on pilgrimage. As is customary, one has to give up something for God. He prays, "Lord, from this day, I give up eating bitter gourd." Swami laughs as he says, "You don't like it anyway, so that is not sacrifice!" The vacation and spending time at home with my parents was definitely very dear to me. And so, I was convinced that it was indeed a sacrifice I was making for something I loved more - i.e. Swami's physical interaction.

The Holidays

The holidays began on the 20th of October (1998) and were to last for about ten days. By the end of the first day itself, the school hostel was almost empty. There might have been only about thirty students staying back - less than 10% of our total hostel strength. Among the thirty too, about fifteen of the students had stayed back because their homes were very far off and the time required to travel itself was about 3-4 days, to and fro. I felt quite lonely on the first day as I returned to the hostel in the evening after *darshan*. The wonderful teachers spoke to us and enthused us often. "You are all very special. Everyone stays for Swami when school is on. You have shown that Swami is extra special for you. You too are extra special for Swami." These words encouraged and pumped back enthusiasm into me.

It turned out to be an interesting and fun vacation. We had a couple of picnics to the Chitravati river banks. We played a lot and had daily *darshans*. Most importantly, we got a chance to serve at an eye camp held in *Kottacheruvu*. The alumni of the Institute had organized an eye camp wherein they operated upon dozens of patients for cataracts, free of cost. Since all of the recipients came from very poor families, they did not have the knowledge nor inclination to take post-operative care. We schoolboys got the opportunity to stay with these patients for two days, taking care of their needs till the bandages on the eye came off. All these happened, but I never got any special 'physical interaction' with Swami.

However, deep within, I knew that for all the sacrifices and service that I had done, Swami would definitely reward me. That faith is very important. We may not know how we will be rewarded but we should have faith that none of the good deeds which we do, will ever go unnoticed by the Eternal Witness!

A Pleasant Bolt From The Blue

The reward came - on the 28th of October to be exact. And it happened in a manner that I never imagined. It felt like another normal day in Prasanthi Nilayam. (Today, I know that no day in the Divine presence is ever normal!) Swami completed His *darshan* rounds and called a large group of devotees from some district of Andhra Pradesh for a group interview inside the *bhajan* hall. It was a group of about 75 ladies and 75 gents. The doors and windows of the *bhajan* hall were closed and it was a completely private session for the blessed group. I was among the hundred or so students (from the school and Institute) waiting for the interview to finish. After about half an hour, the interview was over and the devotees began to file out of the *bhajan* hall. One person from the line walked up to me and told me, pointing to my Nikon camera, "Can you come and take a photo of our group?"

I was hesitating. I did not know who this person was. I did not know what I should answer him. He continued, "Swami said that you should take the photo." I was surprised. I nodded. I had a Nikon F90 film camera and I got up with it. The man was happy and he rushed back to the group. The members who had come out of the *bhajan* hall had formed a small group on the gents' side of the Sai Kulwant hall. I began to walk towards the group. I thought that I would take a couple of quick shots and then rush into *bhajan* hall for a good place to sit during *bhajans*. As I was walking towards the group, a sudden hush fell in the entire hall. From a state of randomness and entropy, the hall returned to perfect order. I was taken aback at this sudden silence and turned around. Within a few feet from me was Swami! And He was walking straight towards me!

This was totally unexpected - as unexpected as that person's request to take a photo. I wondered what Swami would tell me for 'loitering' in the hall with a camera. This was a bonus '*darshan*' session which nobody had even dreamed of. So, I simply sat down wherever I was. Swami passed by me without making any comment or even seeing me. I was relieved.

The surprises kept coming. Swami went towards this group (which was seated by now) and told them that He too would stand in the group photograph! The members were simply thrilled. I too was thrilled at this turn of events. I had imagined shooting a picture of a group of men in white. The orange figure in the centre changed everything! As Swami stood with the group, I clicked a couple of pictures. Then, I quickly sat down in my place. I was feeling very special for having got this opportunity to be His photographer but I was also nervous because Swami had not called me directly. As Swami was returning and passing by me, He asked, "College student?" I was still in school. But I simply nodded, "Yes Swami." (I completed my Bachelors and Masters degrees in His college, but that is a different story.) He then told me, "Go to the ladies' side." "He must be joking", I thought. I got up and began to walk behind Him. He again turned around and said, "Go to the ladies' side." I was quite confused and so I walked to the interview room and stood outside there. I thought as Swami returned to the interview room, I would ask Him what He really meant by that message.

The Second Pleasant Bolt From The Blue

As I stood waiting at the interview room, I could see Swami crossing the students' sitting area. Instead of turning towards the interview room, He continued along, into the ladies' side. I was wondering what was happening when He turned and looked at me. "The ladies' side", He signalled. I saw where He was pointing and suddenly, realisation dawned. The women belonging to the group which had received the interview in the *bhajan* hall had also gathered for a group photograph. Swami had been trying to make me understand that I should be ready to take a group photo on the ladies' side also! Was I thrilled! I quickly ran and began to walk beside Swami now. I felt so comfortable and good. It was like walking with my best friend. Today I realise why Swami says, "Do not walk in front of me; I may not follow you. Do not walk behind me; I may not lead you. Walk by my side; Be my friend."

The ladies' group was seated and it seemed much larger than the gents' group. Swami stood in front of all the seated ladies and told me to take a picture. I saw through the lens that the whole group was not getting covered. My lens was not wide enough. And I could not move back any further for all the other ladies devotees were seated there. Even as I was wondering what to do, Swami called out to me and said, "Go more back." I was thinking, "I know Swami! But how?" The minute Swami told me to move back, all the ladies behind me saw His action. They instantly parted to create a way for me! Ah! Another lesson here - when the Lord gives you a task, He also gives you the ability to complete the same. I took the picture and was happy with that. Swami then told me to move to another angle and take a picture from there also. Again, the same treatment followed - the ladies made way for me to move and take a position from where I could cover the whole group.

As the picture was taken, Swami moved back towards the interview room. I followed Him there. Just before He entered the interview room, He looked at me, smiled and asked, "What are you still following me for? Go and sit in your place." Ah! What a smile it was! I floated back to my place with the students. Everyone seemed amazed at what had happened in the last fifteen minutes or so. Those around me were asking me about how Swami chose me and what He spoke with me. I was feeling very special and this added attention made me feel even more elated.

The Subtle Working Of The Ego

After the *mandir* session in the evening, I returned to hostel. I had no idea what to do next when our mathematics teacher,

Sri.Venkateswarlu, called me. He explained to me, "This is a great chance that we in the school hostel have got to serve Swami through you. We should get those negatives developed and print photographs - as many copies as there are people in the group. I shall get it done for you." I accepted his loving offer. I rewound the film roll and gave it to him. I walked out of his room and soon realised that I was the talk of the hostel. All the students smiled at me as I passed them. The teachers too smiled at me. That felt so great. Unknown to me, my ego had raised its ugly hood already and I was foolishly relishing that! The next day, Venkateswarlu Sir summoned me again to his room. He handed over to me about 150 prints - one for each person in the group-- and said in all humility, "Am grateful to Swami for having given me this chance to serve Him in a little way. If tomorrow, Swami asks you as to who paid to get the photos printed, tell Him that all the teachers did it as a mark of gratitude to Him." Instead of being impressed at the humility of this person and his love for Swami, I was lost in thoughts of myself! "Surely Sir. When Swami calls me today, I shall tell Him what you said." I had fatally assumed that I would be called! That was not all. Another teacher, Satish Babu Sir, called me to his room. He lovingly wrapped all the photographs and tied them up in very decorative ribbon. "Am grateful to be able to play a small role in this offering to Swami", was his statement. I had forgotten that all this attention and love was because of Swami and I was only an instrument. I assumed a huge sense of self-importance. I dug deeper into my 'ego pit' when I jocularly remarked to a classmate, "If you want a close *darshan* of Swami, sit by my side. When He talks to me, you can even take *padanamaskar.*"

The Fall

Armed with two bundles of photographs, I made my way to the *mandir.* I was very excited. It was the 29th of October, 1998 and I was sure that it would be a red-letter day in my life. I was seated in the first line and was sure to be in Swami's path when He came for *darshan.* Soon, the music came on and a hush fell over the hall. Swami glided in majestically into the Sai Kulwant Hall. I quickly straightened my sleeves and adjusted my hair. I gently aligned the ribbon on the 'gift' that I would be presenting to Him. To my great disappointment and chagrin, Swami walked almost till me, and as He was about to come in front of me, turned away and walked towards the devotees sitting on the other side. Having passed me, He again returned to my side and stayed on the same side almost throughout the line! I was stunned. I was in a state of utter disbelief. Adding salt on the wounds of my ego was the boy by my side, "You know what! Had I sat anywhere else other than next to you, I would have got a *padanamaskar.*" He got up that instant and moved to a more 'Swami-friendly' spot. The amount of show I had indulged in without my knowledge made almost all the students (there were very few who had stayed back during the vacation) look at me in almost a questioning way, "What happened to Swami taking the photos from you?"

From The Peak Into The Nadir

I was instantly dejected. I wanted to run away, hide from all and cry. But I was in the *mandir* and there was no place to go. I got an idea. I got up and went to the *mandir* portico where only the VIPs and birthday students sat. This area was right opposite to the interview room. I sat behind a pillar there. The space was empty because this spot was completely shielded by the pillar and though one could sit there to be physically close to Swami, one could not see Swami even though He was a few feet away. That was a perfect spot for me. I could sit there, hiding from everyone, including Swami, and mourn as much as I wanted. The mourning turned into self-criticism and self-abasement in no time. "You are an egoistic pig", I told myself, "And you will never get close to the Lord. You have no virtues and even when Swami gives you a chance to get close to Him, you fritter away that opportunity with your stupid pride. You are good for nothing. You are not fit to even show your face to Swami or see Swami." This hammering went on. Now, the reader will know that such criticism is dangerous - akin to cursing oneself because what you hold within is what you get in life! But well, I went on and on. My face was hot and I was quivering with sorrow and dejection.

The Upliftment

Things happened so suddenly. Swami would come often into the portico from the interview room and interact with people there. He had come out now and was speaking to the Warden of the Institute hostel. I moved slightly out of my corner so that I could see Him and He could see me ("If I deserved so", as I thought at that time.) When I moved, the plastic bag on my lap also moved and made a rustling sound. Swami heard that, looked at me and asked, "What is there in that cover?" "Swami, photos... yesterday's photos...", I answered in a feeble tone. Swami's face suddenly seemed to light up. He made an expression saying, "Oh! How could I forget!" He called out to me. I got up from my place and walked to Him. I offered the photos to Him and said, again in a feeble voice, "Swami, this is the gents' group and this is the ladies' group." He gave them back to me and beckoned me to follow Him. Thus it was that I walked behind Him for the second time in 2 days. He led me out in public, on to the central dais. From there, He beckoned to the main coordinator of yesterday's group. He came rushing to the dias. Swami took the gents' bundle and handing it over to him said, "This are the photos of the gents", and looked at me asking, "Right, isn't it?" I just nodded. Then He did the same procedure with the ladies' bundle too. The coordinator thanked Swami but asked, "Swami, can I have the negatives?" Swami turned and looked at me. As advised by my teachers, I had cut out those negatives and had carried them in my pocket. I fished them out and gave it to Him.

"Good boy, good boy", He said and I felt a burden lift off my heart. He then told me to take *padanamaskar* in full public view. Then He told me to return to my place. Even as I returned, a student tapped me and said, "You are very special. Swami loves you so much." I smiled to myself. I was not going to go down that road again. "We are all special. Swami loves us all very much. It is just that today He gave me an opportunity. I am grateful."

Chapter Ten

Nourishing My Blood With His Love - The Haemometer Episode

In an interesting episode, I learned another beautiful facet about my God - that nothing is "too big" or "too trivial" for Him. What is "big" for me, however miniscule or trivial it may seem to the world, is "big" for Him too. It was such experiences that made Swami my best friend and fostered my faith in Him. I was studying 11th grade. It was in the year 1998. I was relatively new to the concept of being a student. I had only one desire in my heart - to go near to Swami and become dear to Him. The journey had been quite eventful till then and it promised to get better and more profound. Every day, new concepts about God in general and Swami in specific were formed in me and old ones demolished. On the 22nd of July, 1998, I got a chance to experience His all-knowing nature, once again.

Before I dive into the happenings on that day, a brief note on faith. When it comes to matters of faith, Swami has always been very scientific. He says, "Come, see for yourself, experience and then develop faith." Testing is allowed and the Lord is more than willing to undergo such tests by students, devotees and new comers. But He expects the tester to be scientific in accepting the results as well. Once something is proved, one is expected to develop faith. And that I think is not a huge ask.

For instance, when cars are crash-tested, it is not done on each and every car, every time. Once a car has withstood the crash-test, it is taken on faith that all the other cars too, are strong. People just go ahead and drive knowing that in case of an accident, their car will stand by them. But with God, everyone seems to want to experience everything and then only think about faith. Swami encourages that, nevertheless. All He asks is, once you have experienced, develop faith. Do not get carried away by what others say or do, for is it not your own experience?.

Biology Practicals – My Introduction To The Haemometer

Returning to the episode, the story begins in the post-lunch session of the classes. It was the biology practicals class and we were doing an experiment entitled - Haemometer. The haemometer is a compact device to measure the haemoglobin levels in the blood. It is reliable and simple and consists of diluting one's blood sample with distilled water till its color matches the color of a standard solution provided.

There was one classmate of mine whose physical structure was of a small build. He was the first to do the test and his haemoglobin levels were detected to be around 14.8. Our teacher said that this was excellent. He then told us that for women a reading between 11 and14 was good and, for men, it was 12 and16. I thought, "If this puny guy has 14.8, my reading should be quite high." Eager to find out my haemoglobin levels, I did the test. To my shock, it showed 11.6 - the least in the entire class of 14. And I was the only one who did not seem to qualify being a 'man' as far as haemoglobin levels were concerned! (Well, I have a slightly lesser haemoglobin count which the doctor has told me is perfectly normal in my case. It affects me in no way and so, I have accepted it now. I take no medication or eat any special diet for it. But back then, I thought I had some serious disease or affliction!)

The bad news was that the bell rang and the teacher did not have enough time to explain what the results meant. I was very worried. I told one of my friends that my haemometer might be problematic. We re-did the test. And the result was worse than before - 11.4! I mentally thought that with every passing minute, my haemoglobin was dying away! (Feel like laughing about it now that a sampling error made me feel that I was going to die.) As we walked back to the hostel, I was lost in thoughts. How was I to tell my parents that I seem to be suffering from some strange condition or disease? They would get scared. But I too was scared. I turned to Swami. I prayed, "Swami, my haemoglobin levels are low and seem to be falling. Am I going to die? I don't want to. I want this life so that I can get close to you. Please give me *vibhuti* and cure this ailment of mine."

When I reached the hostel, everyone was talking about inviting Swami to the hostel. In fact, that had been the 'happening' thing in the hostel for the past one week. For the hostel anniversary, the students wanted Swami to come to hostel and everyone wrote letters, made cards and prayed verbally for the same. Today, a concerted effort along all fronts had been planned.

I joined the lines to the *mandir*. I carried a letter in my hand and a prayer in my heart. The letter and prayer were both not for His arrival to the hostel (what if I was not healthy enough to witness that?), but for my health. When we reached the Sai Kulwant hall, we saw that the students from the Institute had not yet arrived. As we were entering the *mandir*, the music filled the air and Swami glided out for *darshan*. *Darshan* was an ethereal experience (like always!). But those days, the *Darshan* had a distinct flavour of its own.

Since the huge marbled area in the centre of the hall was unoccupied, we rushed in and filled up the spaces meant for the Institute students. Today seemed to be a lucky day and many of us got to sit in the first lines. As Swami neared us, I thought of going up on my knees and asking for *vibhuti*. But, sadly for me, the theme of that day seemed to be Swami's visit to the hostel. Everyone who rose to speak with Him, only asked about His visit to the hostel. Swami kept walking and I did not deem it right to place my personal agenda before the hostel agenda. And so, when He came right in front of me, I got up and said, "Swami please come to the hostel."

Swami's reply was, "Tomorrow, tomorrow..." He moved on and I sat back. My medical letter remained in my pocket and the tragedy that I thought I was undergoing outweighed the joy of having spoken a few words with Him. Swami moved a little ahead and I saw that He was circling His palm. He was creating *vibhuti* for some devotee.

I had seen Swami give Vibhuthi to boys for apparently trivial reasons too. I felt my problem was definitely big enough to warrant some vibhuthi.

As I saw Swami twirling His palm, I rushed to Him. Swami gave the *vibhuti* to the devotee. Then, He looked at me, kneeling by His side with a handkerchief in my hand. That look simply melted me. I wished I could merge in Him at that very instant. Much to my surprise, I found myself speaking in a mesmerised tone. As I offered the handkerchief, I said three words, " I love you."

How else could I tell what was going on in me? If my 'disease' got worse and I would not be allowed to stay in the school and hostel, that was as good as death for me. So I thought that the most important thing to do was to tell Swami that I loved Him. Swami response was also in three words, "Po, Po, Po" (meaning, "Go, Go, Go"). I returned to my place. A tear was forming in my eye. When you tell someone that you love them, you expect them to reciprocate. I did not think Swami would respond in this manner. As I bent my head down, tears simply streamed from my eyes. No! They were not tears of sorrow. They were tears of joy because I saw Swami's response.

Instead of wiping His hand on the kerchief, He had wiped the entire vibhuti on to the top of my hand! I do not know how that *vibhuti* changed my haemoglobin levels. But it instantly shot up my love levels for Him.

Chapter Eleven

Love Is God's Only Weakness...
And Our Only Strength

Shift In The Darshan Venue

As I turn the pages in the book of my life as a student of Swami, I arrive at an episode that shows both - how one should win God and how one should not! Both are important lessons and once they are learnt, why would one want anything else? The episode took place over a period of a few months but it felt as if it spanned years. Talk about relativity of time! Time seems to slow down infinitely when you are eagerly waiting for something to happen and are spending agonizsing time in that anticipation.

It was the year 1999. It was the year when some Italian devotees, as an expression of love for Swami, wanted to cover the roof of the Sai Kulwant hall with the thin, gold foil that now adorns the majestic hall. Swami was happy because the roof above the devotees would be covered in gold. He blessed the project and it began in right earnest. Please allow me to take a little detour here and re-live a wonderful story I heard from Ms.Moiya, the famous younger twin of the Pink sisters (the O'Brien twins from Australia), during an interview for Radiosai. She narrated an interesting experience amidst the interview and I quote her:

Well, some years ago a man came to our door and we gave him one of our books. And he came back the next day and said, "Look, you don't even know me and you gave me that book, so I'm going to tell you a story which not many people know." And then he said, "You know the story of the green ceiling? Baba sent for me, I come from Hyderabad." And He said, "I have got a special project for you. The Italian people want to put gold leaf on the upper part of the ceiling. So we got to put a background, I want you to supervise it." So they got coloured charts with all the pinks and the blues and the cream, and Baba said, "No, no I don't want that - I want green." "Oh no Baba, green would clash; it doesn't go with the other colours, it must be one of these colours." "No, I want green," Baba said and continued, "You know those green and gold rings I give people for love, peace and healing? I can't give everybody a green and gold ring but if I give them a green and gold ceiling, anybody who sits under that ceiling will get the benefit. The energy will fall on them even if they are not aware of it; they will get that energy."

When the work of pasting the gold foil leaves on the ceiling began, the venue for *darshan* and *bhajan* was shifted from the Sai Kulwant hall to the adjacent Poornachandra auditorium (PC). So, when the academic year began in June 1999, we were told that we would be going for *darshan* into the PC. I had a photograph with me - it was a 30 inches by 40 inches image of Swami seated on the chair on the *Shivaratri* morning which I had clicked a few months before. My desire was that Swami should sign this photograph so that I could keep it in my shrine at home.

Attempts At Fulfilling A Desire...

Being a student in Swami's school availed some terrific privileges. One of them was the 'birthday tray' chance. If it was your birthday, you would get a chance to sit in the front rows with a tray filled with various goodies. These would include chocolates, dry fruits, cloves (which Swami loved and would pop into His mouth once in a while), *vibhuti* packets, photographs, pens, books - basically, whatever one wanted to take! Swami would bless the student and many times, even sign the photographs presented. I decided to get the photo signed on my birthday, the 24th of June, when Swami would be 'obliged' to sign it for me!

Well, this was not the first time that I was making such assumptions. I had done it once before, when it turned out to be my first memorable interaction with Him as His student. That had made me bold into making more such assumptions... When the D-day came, I went to the Warden and took a 'chit' - a permission slip to go to the *mandir* before the lines left hostel. These chits were given as special considerations for birthday boys or to those that had to urgently communicate to Swami about some matter. Leaving the hostel before the lines gave one the option of choosing the best and prime seating locations in the *mandir*, which had a 'greater chance to access Swami'! And so, on my birthday, I rushed to PC and sat in the first line, just below the stage. I was surrounded by other birthday boys. Swami arrived for *darshan* and I had an eager anticipation about me.

The side curtains marking the backstage area in PC would part and the beloved form in orange would arrive. Immediately, the music would begin and an enthralled hush would fall over the whole audience. There would be many people stranded outside the auditorium for the capacity of PC is only half of that of Sai Kulwant hall. Swami descended the stage and came straight towards us. He placed His right palm on all our trays and allowed us to bow down, touch His feet and take *padanamaskar.* And then came the time to get the photos signed. Swami took the picture that one of the students held and signed it. In the meanwhile, I quickly unrolled the large photograph that I had with me. Swami signed two more photos and then came to mine. I handed Him the marker pen. He took it and just placed it on the photo. And then, I got a shock! He replaced the cap on the pen, gave it to me and just walked away without signing the picture! I felt cheated! Every birthday boy had got his picture signed and only mine had resigned. But I did not give up. The next day, I took a 'chit' in the 'photos for signing' category and again went ahead in the lines. I rushed and procured a place near the birthday boys. When Swami came near during the *darshan*, He signed some photos and then, looked at me and said,

"Only birthday boys!"

He moved on without signing the photo I had in hand. I was flabbergasted! Again, not a person to give up easily, I began to take permission chits to go ahead of lines till the Warden himself got irritated at my frequency. He told me,

"You wait for a while and try your luck again after a few days. There are many boys who want a chance and it is not right that you go ahead daily and sit in the front." When this happened, I was lost in introspection. I began to wonder what was happening and why was it that my photo was not getting Swami's sign? And then, I made a plan - my master-plan! I began prayers on a daily basis. I prayed,

"Swami, please accept a letter from me..."

My Cunning Plan To 'Trap' Swami...

I felt that if I pleaded and prayed enough, Swami would indeed accept my letter. This prayer went on for weeks when finally I reached a state of being where I felt that Swami would never refuse a letter from me. That day, I sat in the second line behind the birthday boys, below the PC stage. This time, I had obtained that seat through dint of hard running and crafty overtaking! I began to write my letter. I wrote asking for His love and blessings. I prayed for my family and for me to be with Him always. And then, I added a post script. I wrote-

"P.S. - Swami if you accept this letter from me, it means that when I get a photo tomorrow and sit in the first row, tomorrow itself You will sign it."

"There", I thought, "this is an intelligently designed, foolproof plan." When Swami came, I was sure that He would accept my letter and He sure did.

"Trapped you", I thought with a triumphant smile beaming on my face.

And so, the next day, I got ready for *darshan* in a great hurry. Swami has 'Sathya' in His name itself. He always utters the truth and so, there is no way He can escape the plot that I have so intelligently weaved! Suddenly, I realizsed that the XII class students would be going last in the lines that day. How was I to get the photo to Swami if I do not get to sit in the front line? I had to complete my end of the deal before expecting Him to keep up His! I rushed to the Warden.

"Sir, I would like to take a chit today."

"For what?"

"Sir, I want to get a photo blessed and signed by Swami..."

"Oh! That same photo! Again?! Just wait a few more days..."

"No! Please sir. I have to take it today."

"See boy, Swami has not been signing photos for the last few days. Let Him start signing and then you take it."

I did not want Swami to escape in this manner. I tried my last card.

"Sir, I have a strong feeling He will sign the photo today. Please, give me a chit."

"I feel, He will not do so. Wait for a few more days."

"Sir...", even as I began, the Warden thundered, "I told you already! Now leave! Do you know better or I?"

I had half a mind to say that I knew better but I knew better than to talk that way to an infuriated Warden. And so, I returned and joined the lines. Swami seemed to have defeated me.

Allow me another little, necessary detour. Those days, Swami would often go to the SaiKulwant Hall before *darshan* in PC to supervise the gold foil pasting work that was going on. On the route that the students took to enter PC, the path connecting Sai Kulwant hall to PC lay. Thus, when we would go for *darshan*, if Swami happened to be in Sai Kulwant hall, supervising the work, we would obtain a bonus *darshan*. There was also an added rule – since the class arriving last to PC would not get good seating, the boys could sit along the path and enjoy a close *darshan* as Swami moved from Sai Kulwant hall to PC.

The day our class was last and I was ruing my inability to sit with the photo in the front line, Swami had gone to Sai Kulwant hall for supervision. Being last, all our class boys sat along the path on one side. On the other side sat the students from the University class that was last in the University lines. I happened to sit in the first line along Swami's path and with great disappointment I realized that I had not brought the photo! How could I have blundered?

I was again lost in introspection. This time it was deeper. I realizsed my mistake. I had been so wrong in planning this 'trap'. I decided to make amends. I took another piece of paper and began to write a letter to Swami. I came straight to the point, "Swami, I am sorry I made a mistake in the previous letter. If you take this letter from me, it means that within the next month, you will sign the photo for me when I sit in the first line!"

That was the gist of the letter and now I felt that this was a perfectly fool proof plan. Within a month, surely I would get to sit in the first row with the photo. Now, I was fervently hoping and praying that Swami would accept my letter...

Does The Second Hatched Plan Succeed?

Now, I was fervently hoping and praying that Swami would accept my letter. As Swami completed the supervision and was returning, He saw all of us seated along the path. He said out loud, "I shall go to PC from the other path!"

"NOOO SWAMIIIIIIIIII......" we screamed at the top of our voices.

"To avoid me, He is going by another path", I thought. "SWAMI, PLEASEEEEE SWAMI" – another shout reverberated.

Swami smiled and turned to enter our path. I heaved a sigh of relief. As Swami came near, I did something very brave and desperate. I got up and blocked His path with the intention of not letting Him pass till He took my letter. He looked at me and said, *"Dunnapota"* (meaning he-buffalo in Telugu). I was thinking, "Call me all you want Swami. I am not budging till you take this letter."

He had about twenty letters in His hand already. Still, He took mine and then I 'allowed' Him to pass. I was happy and relieved. Swami then moved slowly through all the boys, collecting almost all their letters. By the time He reached near the entrance of His residence, behind PC, His hands were full of letters. He went into the door and the door closed behind Him. All of us immediately rose to rush into PC for Swami would be arriving there in about 5-10 minutes. As we were all getting up, one of Swami's security guards came calling out to all of us.

He said that as Swami was entering the door, He had dropped one letter and then gone in, closing the door. Even as He said that, I had a sinking feeling in my stomach. I went to the door and there lay my letter! It had been cast out – a refugee that sought to get back into my pocket. I felt like a fool and began to tear the letter. A senior patted me on the back and tried to help saying, "Brother! The letter has been folded too small. Maybe, it slipped out of Swami's hand. Try again later. Swami will take it." I was in no mood to listen. I had been defeated in a smashing manner. After that day, somehow or the other, I never took that photo for signing.

The Climax?

A month or two passed. The work in Sai Kulwant hall was complete and it was reinstated as the *darshan* venue. My photo was still unsigned and I gave up on that idea totally. So many things happened in the months that passed – many experiences, many lessons. Now let us fast forward to January 2000. The Sports Meet had concluded and I had been able to capture one lovely picture of

Swami smiling and blessing the crowds that had gathered. The desire to get a photo signed by Swami re-ignited with this photograph.

The birthday boys now sat in the lower veranda of the *bhajan* hall, just outside the interview room. Since I was a photographer, many students who were celebrating their birthdays took a permission chit for me too so that I would capture the special moments when they were being blessed. I carried a series of six photographs with the objective of getting them signed at least now. And then began the next part of the struggle. Swami would sign photographs about twice a week on an average. But every time I thrust my photo, Swami would say, "Ay! Not birthday boy." This became so frequent that the student who used to walk behind Swami, one day reprimanded me, "Do not keep bothering Swami daily like this. If you do so, I will ensure that you are not sitting here!"

"As if His neglect was not enough, He was releasing His 'goons' on me", I thought! I suddenly felt the futility of all my efforts. I just prayed to Him saying that I was ready to wait until He signed my photograph at His pleasure. The month changed into February and I continued to sit near the birthday boys, taking their pictures as Swami blessed them, hoping that one day He would sign my photograph. By now, I had dropped most of the photos and was carrying only the photo of His Sports Meet blessing with me. It was a small 7 inches by 5 inches picture.

On the 8th of February, 2000, Swami completed the *darshan* rounds and arrived into the veranda of the *bhajan* hall. There were two tiny tots from the primary school and Swami was so happy seeing them. One of them gave Him a picture to sign and Swami happily took the picture and signed it. And then, He asked, "Only one photo?"

The little guy turned the pages of a book he had got and pulled out a photograph. Swami took that and signed it and I thought, "You lucky fellow!" "Only two photos?" Swami asked, liberally sprinkling divine salt on my ego wounds. Now the little guy rummaged his pockets and pulled out a small, crumpled picture. Swami took that and signed it too!

I was wondering, *"Mera number kab aayega* (When will my time come?)" I sat still. Swami took a couple of steps near me. The pen was still in His hand and He was looking at me. I was tempted to rise but the look of Swami's 'goon' behind pressed me back to my seat. And then, He spoke,

"Don't you want to get your photo signed?" Like a coiled spring, I surged ahead and gave Him the photo. He smiled and said that if only I had brought a writing pad along, photo signing would have been so much easier. I had been getting the writing pad and a book almost daily and today was the only day I had forgotten!

Swami then supported the photo on His left forearm and signed, "With Love Baba". Then looked at me and asked with His eyes, "Only one?" I nodded for that was the only picture with me. He handed the picture to me and moved into the interview room. I looked at the 'goon' and He was smiling broadly at me. I felt so happy! The wait now seemed worth every single moment. I vowed never to try to outsmart God! Just love Him and He will oblige and do what is best for me always.

Another Climax – Dated 15th March 2012

The photo that Swami signed for me is in my altar, laminated. A few years ago, it had fallen on to the lamp and part of the photo had got burnt. But, no part of Swami in the picture had been singed. And now, for a super thriller. This article was being written after I had received some harsh criticism from people who said that I should not keep 'doling' out personal stories like this on blogs. I had prayed to Swami and told Him that He knew everything – and that included my motives in writing articles regularly. And then, I started writing this hub. I had just started writing this article when Pooja, my wife called me up excitedly.

She wanted me to rush home from the studio (where I work) immediately. She had started reading the Shirdi Sai Satcharitra on 15ᵗʰ March 2012, a Thursday. On completion of the first chapter, she placed the book down and closed her eyes in love and gratitude to Swami. When she opened her eyes, the book was full of *vibhuti*! I saw the book and was marvelling at it. I told her that her reading had indeed been sanctified.

I went to the altar to thank Swami for that beautiful miracle and lo! There was also *vibhuti* on the very same photo about which I was writing the article! I knew that Swami was happy with me writing this article and with me writing about Him too!

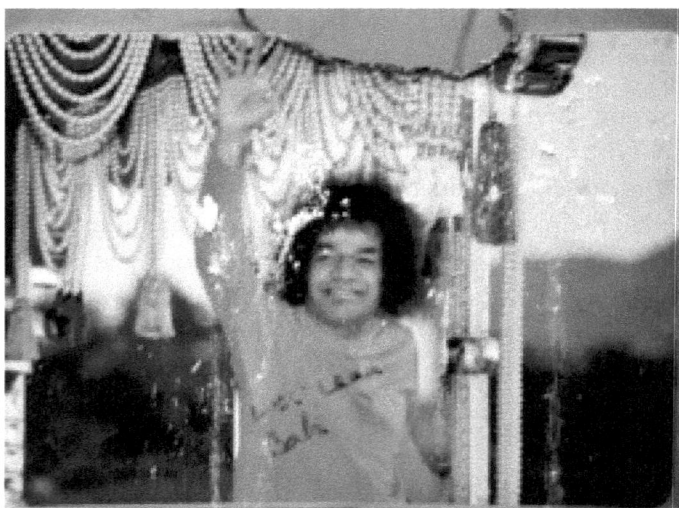

His loving surprise for me in my altar.

Chapter 12

The Day Swami Bled To See
His Children Smile...

Christians often speak about how the saviour, Jesus Christ, bled to save mankind from its sins. Whenever I come across that statement or hear it, my mind races back to the 11th of January, 1999. That is a day etched in my heart coupled with mixed emotions. It is a day whose memory makes me smile and cry at the same time. It is a day when dear Swami bled so that His children could be happy.

I had joined as a student of the XI class in 1998 and I was very excited about participating in my first ever Sports and Cultural Meet of the Sri Sathya Sai Institutions. Each passing day, my relationship with Swami was growing in different dimensions. Ever since that first memorable experience where He accepted my love, I looked forward to each event to add to my experience-bank.

A Sacred Time

The Sports Meet is a time when the students from all the different campuses of the Institute - the Prasanthi Nilayam Campus and Puttaparthi, the Brindavan campus at Bangalore and the women's campus at Anantapur - and the schools at Puttaparthi - Primary school and Higher Secondary school - come together in an effort to please their dear Swami.

The significance of the timing is very profound. It is the time of the *Uttarayana* or the northward movement of the sun. This is considered as a very auspicious time for contemplating on the Lord and it is said that such contemplation leads to oneness with the Lord. In fact, the grandsire in the Mahabharata, Bheeshma, who had a boon that he could die only when he willed, decided to do so in this period of the *Uttarayana*. For the students studying in Swami's schools, thinking of the Lord becomes an automatic affair as they plan and prepare in full gusto for the Sports Meet. As Swami puts it, this is a time when the students bend the body in an attempt to mend the mind and end the senses.

It would suffice here to say this much that students do all sorts of activities - dangerous stunts, dances, drills, displays and, at times, death-defying acrobatics. And they do it with full faith in Swami. It is their way of showing how much they love Him and all that they are ready to do for Him. It is not that Swami ever asks for these expressions of their love. In fact, He is always concerned about their safety and well-being. And that is why He chose to bleed for them...

I remember that day very vividly. As soon as Swami arrived at the Sri Sathya Sai Vidyagiri stadium, a grand and beautiful music filled the stadium. (This was a theme song from a famous movie that had been just released then.) I was seated near the Shanti Vedika, the stage on which Swami would ascend. I was about a good 150 meters away when Swami's chariot entered the ground. I could feel the electric waves of excitement flowing through the atmosphere.

A grand welcome had been planned and the whole procession flagged off in a happy and holy manner at His arrival. I began to focus through my 200mm Tamron lens mounted on the Nikon 801s. Even through the zoom lens, Swami was only an orange speck in the frame. As the chariot moved on, Swami did something that cheered the entire crowd - He stood up in the chariot so that all could see Him properly. Immediately, He became a bigger orange blob in my viewfinder also. I was just focusing and refocusing waiting for Him to fill at least more than one thirds of the frame before I could start exposing the Kodak 200 ISO film that nestled inside. I was just watching and suddenly something terrible happened!

Swami seemed to trip over or something like that and in an instant, the lovable orange figure vanished completely from my viewfinder! I immediately put the camera down and trained my eyes to see what was happening. The chariot had come to a halt but the procession was still moving on, merrily. I understood one dimension of how ignorance could be bliss. Before any worry could envelop the stadium, Swami got up and stood again in the chariot. He was smiling and waving to the crowd as before. I heaved a sigh of relief and picked up the camera, and started shooting away.

The Sports Meet moved ahead with the opening ceremony and the presentations by the various campuses and schools. It was held in two separate sessions - the morning session for two hours and the evening session for two hours. The highlight was when Swami moved down the stage and walked to the field for five times to pose for photographs with the student-performers of the day. There is a reason why I seem to be fast-forwarding all the action of the Sports Meet. I shall return to the events of the day after making a brief visit to the 14th of January, 1999.

Unforgettable Prize Distribution Day

It was Makara Sankranti, the day when the sun actually starts its ascent which is also the day of the prize distribution in Prasanthi Nilayam. That day has held special meaning for me for many reasons. For one, it was on this day that Swami taught me how to walk! But that exciting story is part of another hub.

Swami arrived for *darshan* and completed the prize distribution ceremony. Before Swami's discourse, there was a talk by the then Warden of the Brindavan campus, Sri.B.N.Narasimhamurthy. Even as he came to the podium, he seemed to be sort of overwhelmed. His speech was strange, so to say, in terms of its contents. On such a happy occasion, he began to recollect instances where Swami had taken on the sufferings of His devotees on various occasions. The silencing moment came when he almost broke down while narrating how Swami had suffered a hit to His spine apart from receiving deep gashes on His hand and head when He had the fall from the

chariot on Sports Day! He went on to detail some of the injuries
and how Swami had borne them with a smile. As I sat listening in
the crowd, I felt hot tears stream down my cheeks... Now let us
revisit the 11th of January 1999.

Swami had suffered deep gashes on his back, head and hand.
But immediately, He had 'risen to the occasion' and continued as if
nothing had happened. He had continued to the stage and lit the
lamp and started the proceedings. Though there was excruciating
pain, He had not cared - body attachment is a human quality not of
the divine. It was a miracle in itself that no part of the robe had
torn. It was as if it too shared His divinity.

Then came the part which any human would have found
impossible to bear - to sit through the whole session of about two
hours in such a bleeding and an injured state. We had seen Swami
get up and move backstage very frequently. He did this to wash
away the blood so that nobody noticed. Again, there are students
who maintain Swami's room. Lest they discover about the bleeding,
Swami washed by hand the towels which were blood-stained! And
He did this not once or twice but for more than 5-6 times throughout
the session.

Two students moved to Swami and requested Him to hoist
the flag. That meant another journey of 50 meters or so and He did
it with a smile. The toughest parts were when each campus
completed the presentation and requested Swami to come down to
the ground and grant 'family photographs'!. Shocks of pain must
have shot through Swami's body but He hid it all so well. Calmly,
He moved down for about five times, posing with the children.

Oh! How bad I felt for being part of the huge group that
prayed for Swami to come down! Many times, our prayers are like
that. Having no idea of the past or future, we make our requests
and prayers. And when they get answered, we feel that our prayers
could have been different!

On the 14th of January 1999, Swami rose to deliver His divine discourse. He spoke about the principle of divinity and how God had no body attachment. And then, He stated what He had told Sri.N.Kasturi decades ago - "This body has come for the sake of devotees and shall be utilised for doing anything and everything for their welfare."

The discourse revealed the reasons for the Divine fall. Knowing the past, present and future, Swami had advised the students from the Brindavan campus not to come to Puttaparthi for the Sports Meet. This was a shocker. They prayed and pleaded to Swami to let them come. After much ado, Swami agreed that they could come and perform. However, the stunts that were being performed had been chosen by destiny to deliver some fatal blows. One student had already fallen during the practice sessions and had incurred a serious injury to the spine. The first opinion of the doctor who examined him was that the boy would not be able to sit or stand in his life again. Swami sent *vibhuti* and advised that he should be taken to Bangalore. By the time they reached the hospital, the boy was already sitting! The mercy and love of the Lord brought him out of spinal fractures in miraculous time.

And now, destiny had planned another blow. To avert this disaster and in order to teach everyone the consequences of not listening to Him, Swami decided to take that blow on to His own body. He had silently bled and suffered the pain. But not for a single moment did the pain show on His face. It was an example for all humanity.

Years later, when Swami was in the wheelchair, Prof.Anil Kumar asked Him, "Swami is there no pain?" Swami's response was, "There is tremendous pain. But there is no suffering." And now tell me, how can I not remember Swami whenever I hear that God is sacrificing? His body was like a candle that burned away to provide light for others - a life of great sacrifice.

Swami walked from the stage to the gathering group of
students and back, a distance of two hundred feet,
five times on that day!

Update: Revelations From Other 'Participants' And 'Intimate Observers' Of This Incident..

Brother Nitin Acharya, who had the privilege of serving Swami physically, following Him everywhere, was right by Swami's side on that day. And the story he revealed adds a new dimension to the whole story. Here below is the excerpt as narrated by Brother Nitin –

On 11-Jan -1999 , the sports-meet event took place as usual except for an apparently small 'glitch' right at the beginning, around 7 in the morning. While entering into the stadium, Swami was standing on the silver chariot and waving both His hands and blessing all the devotees assembled in the ladies' side stands. Suddenly, the chariot came to a halt with a small jerk. Swami (seemingly) lost his balance and landed on the seat softly. The seat had been well-cushioned with no sharp carvings or anything that would hurt Swami. We, on Swami's sides, were all-alert and, within moments, Swami was assisted to stand once again. The chariot started it's onward march behind the band boys towards Shanti Vedika, the stage from which Swami and other 'VIPs' watch the sports event.

On the 11-Jan-1999, I believed in what "I saw". As I mentioned earlier, it was just a small episode not worth much attention. It was similar to the experience when we get up from our seat to take the wallet out for a ticket and driver applies brakes and we land on our seat – a momentary embarrassment, nothing more. Then the joyful journey continues. Everyone who assembled there including those who were next to the chariot ignored the same and got engrossed in watching the sports meet. So, initially, I had my doubts when Swami described the whole episode in His Discourse because I had not seen even a single drop of blood on the 11th morning.

Then, came the lesson from none other than Swami Himself. Swami called Narasimhamoorthy Sir (the Warden of the Brindavan campus in those days) inside the interview room. I was about to close the room door from outside when Swami called me too inside. He had already scanned my thoughts and feelings. Warden Sir became emotional and expressed the pain he experienced, after knowing the pain and agony which Swami went through for the sake of a student. This was just one among many such events in the past in the life of Swami. Then Swami looked at me and raised the sleeves of His robe. To my sheer astonishment I saw cuts and gashes deep into the skin with blood clots all over. I was aghast in shock. Swami said "This is just a small fraction. There are wounds, bruises and bandages all over my body. My back bone was in pieces on that day. It would have been fatal for that boy. So, I saved him."

What I was seeing was totally unexpected and against my 'scientific' beliefs. It sent a chill down my spine. His methods are mind-blowing and cannot be comprehended by the five senses of action and perception. I understood that we have to believe in whatever Swami says.

"I am Sathya . Whatever I speak is Truth. Truth, which either happened in the past or would happen certainly in future." Swami is *Trinetradhari* , the one who is three-eyed. He sees the past, present and future which are the three eyes. Swami was the saviour for that boy on that day of 11-Jan-1999. The boy played just a symbolic role. It was a Divine Drama to save the entire humanity.

Brother Asheesh Chopra adds to the above incident:

It is interesting to note that we all see the same event with different perspectives. I had the serving duty and was behind stage that day. We felt we were so lucky that we got multiple opportunities of His Darshan and Swami came backstage to use the washroom. Little did we realise the actual reason which he revealed later – it was to wash / wipe the blood, so that it was not visible to anybody which would make everybody sad.

Chapter 13

The Shivaratri Of My Life...

Speciality Of Shivaratri As A Sai-student

For a student in the educational institutions of Bhagawan Sri Sathya Sai Baba, festivals and celebrations across cultures, religions and nationalities gain significance because Swami emphasises on the religion of love, the caste of humanity, the language of the heart and the omnipresent God, by whatever name you wish to call Him/Her. And based on his/her own inclinations and interests, different festivals fascinate different students who have passed out of the portals of His University. As a student, the most memorable festival and celebration for me was the *MahaShivaratri*.

Lord Shiva is one of the most important Gods in the *Bharatiya* culture and forms an integral part of the holy Trinity as the destroyer - Brahma (the creator) and Lord Vishnu (the sustainer) being the other two. As per the lunar calendar, the 13th night of the waning fortnight is considered as a special night for Lord Shiva - the *Shivaratri* (*Ratri* means night). The 13th night in the month of *Maagha* or *Phalguna* comes once a year and is considered as a special *Shivaratri*, the *MahaShivaratri*.

Massive and magnificent celebrations take place all over India, especially in the northern part of the country which is bordered by the mighty Himalayas. Apart from thousands of temples, the famous shrine, Kedarnath and the devotion-inspiring Mount Kailash with the Manasarovar Lake are located in these Himalayas. However, celebrations at Prasanthi Nilayam, Puttaparthi, which is the abode of Sri Sathya Sai, take on a slightly different flavour. The celebrations there are exactly as dictated by Swami who is widely considered to be a *Shiva-Shakti Avatar*.

Instead of delving into a prose on how the celebrations are different, I feel it would be a much better idea to actually re-live one such special Shivaratri.

This was the *Shivaratri* of 2000 - March 4th, a day I can never forget my entire life. As always, Swami showered such a bounty that raises goose bumps on my entire being in gratitude and wonderment. A little background before the story. I know that whenever I begin like this, there is a danger of the narrative getting very long, but well, that is my weakness. However, let me assure you all that the background will definitely add to the richness of the story. The background will arrive in two parts.

Background - Part 1

I had joined the Sri Sathya Sai Higher Secondary School in 1998. The first Shivaratri I witnessed in the Divine Presence was in the February of 1999. That year, *Shivaratri* happened to fall on the day that is globally chosen to celebrate Love - 14th February. In the morning, all of us students sang songs and *stotrams* in His presence and Swami delivered His Divine Discourse in the evening. Swami spoke on a range of topics from how attachment leads to suffering, how love should be cultivated in one's heart, how one should see only the good in others and never find faults and how one should make Swami as the ideal for all our activities in life. He however, concluded on a note that had not been heard for a long time till then. He said,

Embodiments of Love! As pointed out by the Vice Chancellor in his speech, I used to bring out Atmalingams from this body on the occasion of Shivaratri in the earlier years. Lingodbhava (emergence of Linga from the stomach through the mouth) used to take place on every Shivaratri. To witness this sacred event, lakhs would gather in a small hall. Consequently, there used to be stampede resulting in injuries to devotees. Due to this, I discontinued

Lingodbhava in public. There is a specific time for this. It may take place at any moment between 8 and 10 in the night. It takes place at the right time irrespective of the place I am in. It is bound to take place. It is natural on Shivaratri night. Those who are fortunate to witness this sacred Lingodbhava are freed from all sins. One must see how it emerges. But, some people may not be able to see this even if they are sitting close by. Witnessing the emergence of the Lingam is of utmost importance. Once it emerges, everyone will be able to see it and it has its own benefits. There are many such important aspects attached to this auspicious occasion. You will be immensely benefited if you keep awake and sing the glory of God at least on this night.

That was enough to charge me into full vigour and energy. As far as my memory goes, that is the only *Shivaratri* when I kept awake the whole night singing *bhajans.* The practice among the students in Parthi is a very unique one. They reserve their places with the sitting mats. However, once the place is vacant for more than an hour, it can be moved and taken possession of. So, the whole night, some students keep awake just to displace mats and wend their way to the front lines! I too was among such students. With every passing hour, I progressed ahead, displacing the mats that had been placed there for 'reservation'. It was like the survival of the fittest. As students dropped off to sleep, we conquerors kept awake and surged ahead. By 4am, I had reached the first line! Victory!

Then, something totally unexpected happened. It was past 5:45 am when there were signs of Swami coming for *darshan.* Needless to say, the atmosphere got supercharged with excitement. Swami came straight to the stage and even as He sat there, seemed to be in a sort of discomfort. In a few minutes, He was clutching His throat with two fingers and tears welled in my eyes, seeing Him in pain. Like the others around me, I began to sing the *bhajans* even more loudly. I felt that it was the only way of giving some comfort to Swami. Maybe I could scream so that my throat would hurt instead of His. The situation seemed to only get worse and Swami's body began to quiver and quake, shiver and shake from the pain and effort. And yet, a sweet smile danced on His face. I then remembered having heard about the *Lingodbhava* that Swami used to perform - first from my father and the discourse on the previous evening. I felt that Swami was about to perform the *Lingodbhava*! I looked around and nobody had a camera. Mine was just on my lap! But try as hard as I did, the tears in my eyes did not allow me to shoot! I just watched in awe and wonder as Swami performed the *Lingodbhava*.

In one sudden spasm, Swami moved ahead and from His mouth emerged the golden globule - the *Hiranyagarbha Linga*. And as He picked the *Linga* and exhibited it, I guess I was the only photographer taking pictures. (There was the video camera running however and video stills from the movie flooded the market later on.) In the discourse that followed, Swami said something very poignant.

The principle of Hiranyagarbha is spread all over the body. It assumes a form when I will it. Whoever has seen this Lingam at the time of its emergence till its complete journey outside will not have rebirth. One should see its form as It emerges. In order to sanctify your lives, such sacred manifestations have to be shown to you every now and then. Only then can you understand the divinity in humanity. This Lingam will not break even if it is dropped from a height with force. This is Amritatwam (immortality). It is changeless. You cannot see such a manifestation anywhere else in the world. It is possible only with Divinity.

Needless to say, we were all thrilled. The blessing and bounty was so immense and tremendous. I felt overwhelmed that in my first year as His student itself I had been able to witness the *Lingodbhava*.

*The Lingodbhavam made Shivaratri one of the most austere
and anticipated festivals at Prasanthi Nilayam.*

Background - Part 2

This part of the background is something that I am definitely not proud of. But the need for mentioning it is vital for the story and so I proceed. In the academic year 1999-2000, in grade XII, I got caught when I indulged in an act of indiscipline. The result of that was me getting banned from participating in the Sports and Cultural events and competitions for the academic year. That did not hurt me as much as the other punishment that the Warden awarded me - no permission slips to take camera to the *mandir*!

I felt as if my life support was plucked out. Taking pictures of Swami with the camera had become so much a part of my life that I could not think of sustaining without it. And as *Shivaratri* arrived, I felt that not being allowed to shoot would really become unbearable. I had been eagerly anticipating the *Shivaratri* with the intention of taking pictures of *Lingodbhavam*. And all those hopes were cruelly dashed. I felt cheated! My thinking was that nobody has the right to take someone away from Swami - whatever be his 'crime'. I got angered. I was upset. But I was helpless too. With this background, we now move on to the main story.

Complete Confidence In Swami's Act...

February 2000 was coming to an end and *Shivaratri* was approaching. I was wondering as to how I would be able to take pictures of the *Lingodbhavam*. I kept complaining internally to Swami that I wanted to take photos on *Shivaratri*. Finally, one day before the D day, I wrote a letter to Swami. I do not remember the details but here is the gist which I remember very well. It was this -

Swami! You know how badly I wish to take the Lingodbhavam picture. Now, I am not being given a permission slip to get my camera. Please promise me that if you perform Lingodbhavam this year, I shall get a picture of the Lingam in your mouth.

Armed with this letter, I went and sat in the *mandir*. Swami came and accepted the letter from me. I was so thrilled and happy. I felt that Swami had given me a personal promise. Overnight, my attitude changed from, "I am the unluckiest guy in the hostel" to "Swami will perform *Lingodbhavam* only if I take camera to Mandir." That is the kind of confidence that an assurance from Swami bestows!

The D-day dawned and I went to the Warden's office to request for the camera slip. I was not given permission and I went for the morning session in the *mandir* without my camera. We sang *stotrams* and songs in Swami's presence and it was very uplifting. For the evening session, I hoped that I would get the permission slip though I had no idea as to how that could possibly happen. "If you do not take your camera Aravind, remember that it means there will be no *Lingodbhavam*", I told myself and felt pacified.

Thus, in the evening, I again went sincerely to the Warden's office with the determination to stand there till whatever time necessary. The Warden ignored me and I continued to stand. All the students in the hostel had left for *mandir* and I was maybe the last one still in the hostel. I knew that the Warden would now come on the rounds to ensure that all had left and would drive me out to *mandir*. "He has no idea of the impact of his actions. By denying me a permission slip, he is denying the world of the phenomenon of *Lingodbhavam*" - the heights that the ego can ascend!

As Warden re-entered the hostel, one of the teachers came back to him and said,

"Sir! Today our school boys are chanting Vedas. Please let Aravind take camera so that good photos can be taken when Swami blesses them."

I could not believe my stroke of luck and the Warden could not believe the predicament he had been put into. He was in no mood to let me off the 'punishment' that he had imposed on me. He found a midway solution. He signed a permission slip for me but said,

"This is valid only for today evening. Even if you plan to sit the whole night in the *mandir* for bhajans, make sure that your camera is returned to the hostel." I could sense the disappointment in the heart. The previous year, Swami had performed the *Lingodbhava* early the next morning. If that were to happen this year, I would not be able to take photos! But again I told myself that was not possible because if I did not have camera, then the event could simply not happen!

The Unbelievable Turn Of Events...

I reached the *mandir* with the camera. When some of my friends saw me, their jaws seemed to drop in amazement as to how I managed to get the camera. I simply smiled and moved to the second line and sat. In the meanwhile, Warden arrived and told me, "You need not sit in the front. You have a zoom lens. Sit back and take pictures from there itself." Thus it was that I landed in the 8th or 9th line with a sad face.

The evening proceedings went on fine. There was Veda chanting (how can I forget that which was instrumental in getting me a camera slip!) followed by a couple of speeches after which Swami delivered His divine discourse. Then, the *bhajans* began which would go on throughout the night till the Arati the next day morning. Swami moved into the interview room. My mind was not at all on the *bhajans*. I was going on wondering as to how I would manage to retain my camera till next morning when Swami would do the *Lingodbhavam*. Even as I was furiously thinking thus, Swami arrived out of the interview room. Instead of moving towards His residence, He came to the dais and sat on the chair. This was something new. It was part of His uncertainty that I loved.

As Swami sat on the chair, all of us noticed that He seemed to get spasms in His stomach, chest and throat. I got excited - Swami was going to do the *Lingodbhavam* now! And I had my camera with me. I was so sure of getting a picture of Swami with the *Lingam* in His mouth. As Swami's symptoms progressed, He requested all the photographers in the first two lines to put their cameras down as the flashes were very disturbing. At that instant, I realised why being shunted off to the ninth line was also His blessing. While everyone was made to put down the cameras, I was not told anything since I was so 'far away'!

I knelt down and waited with bated breath for the moment. The spasms became more frequent and intense and my heart was thudding so loud and hard. I knew that the moment would arrive anytime soon. Amidst all that excitement and anticipation, a thought arose in my mind. "Aravind remember what Swami said? *Whoever has seen this Lingam at the time of its emergence till its complete journey outside will not have rebirth. One should see its form as It emerges.* If you try to take a photo, there will be a moment when the shutter closes and you will be cut off from the *Lingodbhavam*. Is it worth sacrificing your liberation for the sake of a picture?"

This thought really disturbed me. And so I did something really crazy. I just focused on Swami and kept my camera to the side of my head. My idea was to simply shoot blind when the moment happened. Within a few minutes it happened. Swami did the *Lingodbhavam* and then even moved amidst the gathered thousands, displaying it for them to see. I shot blindly and since it was the age of film cameras, I had no idea as to whether 'the moment' had been captured.

It was only a week later, when the film rolls were developed by my father in Mumbai, that I got a confirmation of having captured the magical moment. Today, when I think about the probability of getting such an image in the circumstances I was in, I know it is impossible. What a gift Swami had given!

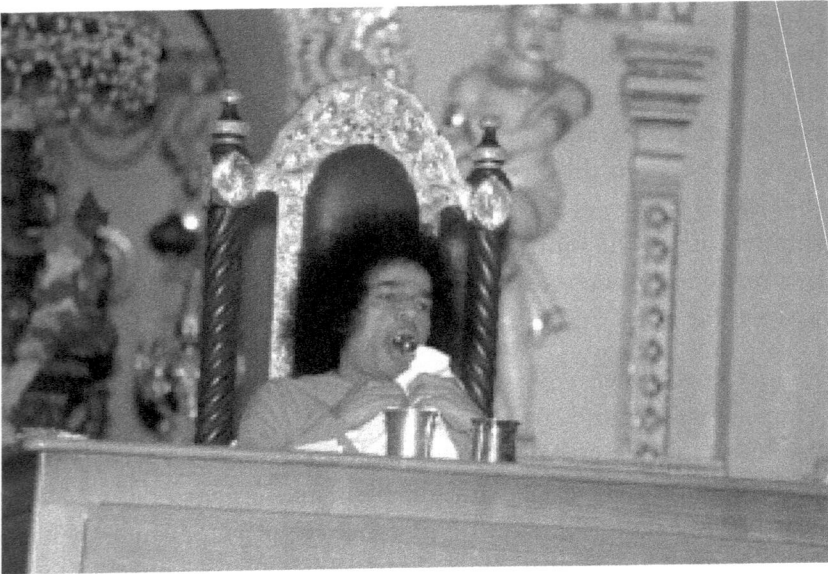

The magical image which Swami granted me that Shivaratri.

I have witnessed at least half a dozen *Lingodbhavams*. I have photographed them with cameras that shoot at 5,7 and 9 frames a second. But I have never managed a photo like that ever. I have also not seen another such photograph anywhere else, taken by anybody else. Of course, there have been video stills made from the films that were shot on those occasions - but no high resolution images. Naturally, for such images cannot be 'taken', they have to be 'given'. This, till date, remains my best *Shivaratri* ever.

I also realise that when it comes to Swami, photos are never 'taken' by the photographer but are always 'given' by the Lord.

Chapter 14

Swami's Delays Are Not His Denials

This is a famous quote that I have heard a million times. Well, not a million times, but it feels like that! It is one of the all-time favourite phrases to be used while consoling someone who is in despair. Even I have made use of it on many occasions - "Hey! Don't worry. Things will sort out. God is there to help. Remember... his delays are not his denials."

When things are sunny and fine, it is easy to state the quote. When things go bad however, we desperately grab on to the same quote and secretly hope in our hearts that this is only a delay and not a denial. Travelling down memory lane, I come across a singular episode that has convinced me beyond doubt that God's delays are definitely not His denials.

Just like a single story of the charming Lord Krishna gets linked to so many other stories which reveal His divine facets, (in fact, deviating from the main story into relevant sub stories has been termed as 'Hari-Katha' in India which literally translates as 'Story of Krishna'!), this story too shall have its sub-stories. But as always, the sub-stories add flavour and spice to the main story. Without any more ado, let us launch into the story.

End Of Schooling – Career Options?

It was the March of the year 2000. I was in 12th grade and was one among a hundred or so preparing furiously for the countrywide Board Examinations. The 12th grade is a transition from high school to University in India and the examinations conducted by the CBSE (Central Board for Secondary Examination) are given paramount importance. For a student in Swami's school, it was a time of a probable, terrible transition. Since Swami had not started any Medical or Engineering colleges and courses for Chartered Accountancy, those wishing to pursue these lucrative and attractive careers had to leave Swami's physical proximity. Having experienced moments of intense Omniscience, one does not want to leave His physical proximity.

Further studies available in the University involved the pursuit of pure sciences and a Bachelors degree in Commerce which are considered pretty 'mediocre' in India. (This is fast changing and the impressive record of the Sathya Sai University has also contributed to it.) Thus it was that a talk given to us by the 'class' teacher, Dr. Sailesh Srivastava became very important and enlightening for all of us students. The talk lasted two hours and was delivered to all of us in the hill-view stadium, one fine evening. It was on the eve of our departure to Brindavan (Whitefield in Bangalore), where Swami had gone. We wanted to seek His blessings as the outgoing batch. The talk that Sailesh Sir gave us was inspirational and full of the divine stories of Swami. One point that he made, struck me and it remains enshrined in my heart to this day.

He said, "Whether we stay with Swami or not is not in our hands. If we are supposed to be away from Swami, even if we complete somersaults to stay on here, it will not be possible. If we are supposed to be here, however hard you try to get away from this place, it will not be possible. So, that is not in our hands. But we can decide what we feel and desire. We can have the intense longing to be with Swami always, irrespective of where life takes us. Take care of your feelings and desires, life will take care of itself." At the end of that talk, everyone wanted to be with Swami, irrespective of what they had originally desired or what their parents had planned. If fate/destiny would take them away, so be it.

Thus it was, that a bunch of highly motivated and charged up students made their way to Brindavan. In the morning, as we all sat for *darshan*, Swami came and made enquiries about how many of us had come and for what reason we had come. The *darshan* got over and we had managed to hand over the bundle of letters that we had all written to Swami. Within a few minutes, we received a word that Swami had called us all into Trayee Brindavan, His residence at Whitefield, for a Trayee session.

A Memorable Trayee Session

With great joy, anticipation and excitement we wended our way into the Trayee compound and entered the hallowed precincts of the building. The *Jhoola* or swing welcomed us and we sat around it. In a few moments, Swami arrived. As soon as He came into the room, He asked, "How many doctors here?" Nobody raised their hands. The speech on the previous evening was obviously showing its effects. Everyone in their hearts was saying, "Swami, we want to be with you." "How many engineers here?" was the next question. Again, nobody raised their hands. Swami put on a surprised expression. Then He broke into a smile and said, "*Anta Gas*" (All gas - meaning lying). All of us shouted loud in unison,

"No Swami! We want to stay with you!"

He seemed pleased by that and then He sat on the *Jhoola*. The session began by us singing songs for Him and He listened to three of them. Swami then began to speak to us. The Warden of the Brindavan campus, Sri. B.N.Narasimhamoorthy, came in to translate. Swami told him that he would not be needed and we were all surprised. We wondered who would be translating then. Swami then told Sailesh Sir to translate what He was saying. It was the most amazing forty minutes as Sailesh Sir, a Delhiite by birth, translated Swami's discourse into English for all of us!

Sailesh Sir translating the discourse made us realise the meaning of being an 'instrument' of the Lord. When God's work is being done, capability, ability and deservedness do not come into picture at all. The Lord achieves all that He wants effortlessly through the instrument. We also began to look up to Sir in a more glorious light and that made us give even more value to the speech he had given us the day before. It was as if Swami was reinforcing it. I remember two episodes that took place distinctly - one that is relevant to the story and the other, which is not but is worth narrating nevertheless. Another advantage of relating apparently 'irrelevant' stories in between the main story is that they can trigger insights and wisdom in the reader which the writer never even felt! The first was that we noticed two small coconut shavings lodged in Swami's hair. One of my classmates, E.Vijay Kumar, got up and told Swami,

"Swami, there is something lodged in your hair." "Is it? Will you remove it then?"

The boy moved further up and tenderly took those two small shavings from Swami's hair. There were smiles all around and the boy treasured them in his pocket. Swami looked into his eyes and smiled. My immediate thought was, "Oh! How I wish I too get a chance to take something out of His hair like that."

The second episode was (the less relevant one) when, in the end, Swami completed the discourse and sat on the *Jhoola* expecting us to make the next move. I asked, "Swami, how should one control anger?" Swami replied, "Ah! Anger. Whenever you get angry, go to the bathroom and open the tap. Try to sing a bhajan in the pitch of the running water. You will cool down. Another option is to immediately see your face in a mirror. It will be distorted and you will see yourself as a primitive monkey. That will bring a smile on your face and dissolve your anger. If nothing works, go and run fast for a furlong. You will be too tired to be angry then!"

The whole session concluded with a group photo with Swami on the Trayee Brindavan stairs. I was not in the picture because I was taking the pictures! It was a very memorable hour and we slowly filed out of the Trayee compound. The Brindavan campus Warden told us later that Swami had been mighty impressed with our batch saying that all wanted to stay with Him. In fact, He had even said that all should be taken into the Institute. All of us were thrilled.

In Trayee Brindavan - asking Swami, "How to control anger?"

How The 'Denial' Proved To Be An Important Lesson

After the Board exams and completion of school, a few boys from our batch did go out for pursuing careers in Medicine, Engineering and other areas. But the majority applied for Bachelor courses in the Sathya Sai University itself. The entrance exams, group discussions and interviews concluded early in May 2000 itself. They had been completed soon because Swami had announced that there would be a Summer Course in Indian Culture and Spirituality for all the students.

When the results were announced, we found out that about 7-8 students had not made it and thus had been denied seats. So, while most of us reported to and joined the hostel at Brindavan, these unfortunate boys felt horribly left out. They went at once to Sailesh Sir and said. "Sir! We wanted to be with Swami but we have not got seats. Should we take this as our destiny and go home and try for further education elsewhere?" Sir's reply was, "In normal circumstances, you could have done so. But Swami was happy and

He said that all must be taken in. So, hold on. Remember, God's delays are not His denials." Ah! There appeared the famous phrase!

Taking heart from what Sailesh Sir had said, the boys waited on. They were no longer recognised as students - they were alumni now. Hence, their preferential seating was also gone and they were sitting with the alumni for daily *darshan*. In the meanwhile, all of us began to attend the auditorium sessions, dining sessions and discourse sessions with Swami daily. When we would meet these 'rejected' and 'dejected' boys, we would not know what to say. Somehow, your fortune appears very mean and bad when presented in front of those from whom that very fortune has been snatched away.

After about four days, 2-3 members from the 'unfortunate' group lost heart and said that they were leaving. If they waited any longer, then their chances of getting a seat into any other university too would be lowered. The others however, held on to the ' Delays are not denials' tagline and prayed. The group, reduced from 8 members to 5, arrived for morning *darshan* on day 6. That day, as Swami was moving around during *darshan*, He 'saw' these boys and asked, "How come young students are sitting in the alumni block?" The boys hurriedly told their predicament to Him. Swami turned around and called the Vice Chancellor. He told him, "These boys must study. They are young to be wasting away like this in the alumni block." The Vice Chancellor just nodded his head. Swami continued, "Interview them and give them seats in our college. Young boys must study!" Two hours later, the group was with us in the hostel shedding tears of joy. They told all of us, "God's delays are not His denials."

A Case Of History Repeating Itself

How many times has Swami said that His word, once given, will always be upheld? In fact, when the Super Specialty Hospital was being constructed at Bangalore, there was a shortage of funds.

Swami was apparently very 'tensed' and 'apprehensive'. He asked a senior, "What should we do? There are no funds."

In an attempt to comfort Swami, the elder said, "Swami! You have promised the world this hospital in one year. The last time you promised, you made the hospital at Puttaparthi and it has been running fine for 10 years now. Just announce that the opening of this hospital will be postponed by a year. People will understand..." Swami looked at Him with compassion and said, "Is this all that you have understood of Swami? I have already said that the hospital will come up. So, now I am helpless. It has no choice but to come up."

The hospital was inaugurated as per schedule. God always steps in, not at the last moment but at the right moment. Fast forward to 2003 summer. Swami got down from the 'golf-cart' vehicle that He often used for *darshan*. I was given the duty of placing the foot stool for Him to use as support. As Swami got down, I noticed a mango flower in His hair. I said, "Swami there is something in your hair." He bent down, smiled and said, "Will you take it out for me?"

Fulfillment of a long cherished desire to touch His hair.

My heart flashed back to the simple prayer that had arisen in my heart, three years ago. As I gently and tenderly plucked the flower from His hair, I realised, once again, that God's delays are not His denials.

And yes!

Those students who were admitted into the undergraduate courses, completed even their Masters course from the same Sri Sathya Sai Institute with flying colours! They did not let Him down...

Chapter 15

The Fruits Of Action

It was the summer of 2002. Like some of the special summers before that, Swami had decided to conduct the Summer Course in Indian Culture and Spirituality. The venue, as always, was the Whitefield Ashram in Bangalore. It turned out to be the most unforgettable Summer Course for me because of the experience it gifted me. Swami used that period to teach me a powerful lesson about who He is. Without spending more time on the suspense build-up, I shall dive into the happenings of that fortnight.

For those that are unaware of what a Summer Course with Sathya Sai Baba is, here is a brief description. It had started off as a study of the Indian Scriptures and value systems for a period of fifteen days for the youth from various parts of India. Swami would take active interest in it and would address the students on a daily basis. The students were also blessed to hear different scholars and erudite speakers. As years passed by, attending a Summer Course was made a special privilege of only the students studying in the various educational institutions started by Swami. The format and schedule remained the same.

The Buddha Poornima celebrations happened towards the fag end of the Summer Course. It was the 26th of May, 2002. I was part of the audio team that arranges mikes for the programmes and ensures good audio from the various speakers hung in the hall. As part of my duty, I was seated right in the front of the hall, with the *bhajan* group. The programmes were being conducted by devotees from Nepal who had filled the Brindavan Ashram. This was a time when Swami had suffered a fall. As a result, two lifts had been erected - one on the ladies' side and one on the gents' side - for Swami to move up and down.

Dilemma Of Duty Vs Discipline

That gave me an added duty. I was told that if Swami goes up the stage by the gents' side lift, the ladies' side lift also should be up just in case Swami decides to use it. This synchronicity of the lifts had not yet been automated. Swami, on that day, completed His *darshan* rounds and moved up the lift from the ladies' side. The lift on the gents' side stayed down. Over the walkie-talkie I got an instruction, "Move to the gents' side and raise the lift up."

I was immediately in a dilemma. I was right in front of Swami. I also had a big camera in hand. Would it not be conspicuous if I rise and go? Would not Swami get upset at my 'indiscipline' of moving during a programme? Even as I was lost in thoughts, I got another message, "The Warden is here. He says that you better go and raise the lift up. In case Swami wants to go down the gents' side, He will be made to wait otherwise."

Now, the Warden of our hostel in Brindavan also happened to be sort of an Administrative Head of the Brindavan Ashram. He was considered as Swami's 'right hand' person to execute various activities. If he was saying, I better do it, I thought. So, I just got up and walked to the lift. I pressed the green button that took the lift up.

Immediately, I felt a hand pull me down. It was a teacher and he seemed upset. He said,

"You fool! Why did you get up and move? Swami was going on seeing you. He does not like such indiscipline. Now, just sit here and don't do anything foolish." I sat down at the lift, a little scared about facing Swami's 'irritation'. But my attention was on my Nikon 801s SLR camera that was on the floor, right in front of Swami. The *bhajans* were on and everyone was singing out loud. The Buddhist devotees sitting there were lost in the ecstasy of devotion and I was more worried. One swipe of an excited limb and my camera would be history! I sat with bated breath, waiting for the programme to conclude.

About half an hour later, Swami gently rose and received Arati. The final Arati song was sung and He moved towards the lift. It was the one on the ladies' side itself. As He moved down, in accordance to the policy, I lowered the lift on the gents' side also. (This was in case Swami wanted to move up the lift again, from the gents' side!) Swami instead, walked in the opposite direction towards the ladies' side corner. From there He was about to exit the hall. At this time, I got up from my place and rushed back in order to safeguard the camera. And then, it happened...

Unexpected Fury

Swami was a good 25 meters away. But, even from that distance, He seemed to see me. He re-entered the Sai Ramesh hall and came walking straight towards me. (I immediately remembered the words of my teacher who had advised me to remain seated near the lift.) For the first time in my life, I had trepidation as Swami was coming near me. He was smiling and blessing the Nepalese devotees who had gathered. Seeing His smiling face, I felt slightly better. But as He came two feet away from me, His expression changed.

His face became red in anger almost instantly. He told me to get up and I rose on my knees. I received full 'fury' on my face. "Are you a student?! Totally indisciplined! You are moving around like dogs and pigs do!" Even as He was scolding me, I felt His saliva on my face - such was the fury. I was totally confused and I stammered, "Swami...er...Warden....lift..." "Yes! Warden! I shall throw you out. I don't want a student like this."

Immediately after this, He looked at the devotees over my head and gave them a broad smile. The red face was gone and so was the fury. I am sure that none of the devotees even made out anything other than the fact that Swami had told me something. He just turned and walked away. I was trembling in fear. I was so shocked and I had never seen Swami in that form ever. Even as Swami was exiting the hall, all the devotees gathered around me. Not aware of what had happened, they were congratulating me.

"You are so blessed that Swami came all the way for you!" "Can you share what was that special secret that He came to share with you?" I was lost for words. I was in tears.

"He is so overwhelmed! Leave him for a while to absorb the beauty of the experience!" I just arose from my place and picking up the mikes, took them to the audio room that was backstage. From the room, I could see and even hear Swami moving towards His residence. The Warden was there. As Swami neared him, he was all smiles. But I could see the smile fading into a grim expression and from that I could guess Swami's expression.

Then, I heard Swami. "That boy....About this tall.....He has a camera.....Is he a student?" "Swami....I shall find out...." (I knew that Warden, from his previous such experience was simply playing it safe)

"Get him here this afternoon. I shall throw him out. I don't want such boys." And Swami walked into the residence.

I returned to my room and was simply lost. I was in a daze and was thinking of what I would do now. In a few minutes, I was summoned to the Warden's office. I walked to the room and saw that the Warden was meeting with some 'big' people. The minute he saw me, he dismissed everyone else and called me in. Somehow, this kind of VIP treatment at this juncture scared me even more. "Boy! What did you do? How could you do such a thing?" "Sir! You told me to go and raise the lift and I did as you said." "If I tell you to jump in a well, will you do it? You should have told me about your predicament and used your common sense!" "What should I do now sir?" "Swami has told me to take you to Him this afternoon and He wants to personally throw you out. Only prayer can save you. Keep praying."

I felt like falling at Warden's feet and asking him to save me! I was like a drowning man clutching at the floating straws. I did not fall at his feet but asked him to save me nevertheless. "Listen to me. Stand in a corner hidden from Swami's view. Pray to Him that He does not notice you. Also pray that when He sees me, He does not ask about you. Only prayer can save you." I accepted what he said and slowly trudged back to my room. I just had tears and was also angry in part. "I just obeyed my elders! Does not Swami know what I was doing? Why did He scold me that way? And now, if I am thrown out after my undergraduate course, what should I do next?" With a loud thudding of my heart, I lay down on my bed.

I had fallen asleep and the time flew by quickly. It was lunchtime. I had no appetite but still ate thinking that if it was to be my last meal in the hostel, it might as well be a good one! Soon, it was 3pm and I did not even want to go near the Trayee Brindavan (Swami's residence) area. All my life I had been seeking His physical attention and now, when I was getting it, I seemed to be shrinking away! I decided that I would not go near the residence in any way. I would seat myself in the hall, as inconspicuously as possible. And yes! I prayed.

In the evening, after the *darshan* and *bhajan* session was over, I wended my way back to the hostel - happy that no summons had come till then; scared that the summons could come anytime now. The Warden came to the hostel and sent for me first thing. He had a nice smile on his face and he told me, "Your prayers seem to have worked. Swami did not ask for you! Congratulations..." I was also relived and was about to celebrate when the Warden continued, "However, we should not take any chances. Do not be seen by Him anytime, anywhere. Do you agree?" As if I had any choice! "If you want to be sure that you don't get thrown out, listen to me. Be last in every line. Never bring yourself into Swami's sight."

A Most Painful Period

This is the worst torture that any student could be punished with - to make efforts to stay away from Swami! But I seemed to be in a really tight spot. If I did not obey and comply, I might have to leave Swami forever. Thus, I agreed and special instructions were given to the 'line leaders' to make sure I was the last student in the last line that moved for *darshan* and *bhajan*.

During the summer course, as I mentioned earlier, there are students from all the campuses. So I was the last, not among the usual 300, but among about 800 students! I lost the motivation and energy to get ready quickly and wait for *darshan* - I would anyway be the last one. The loss of motivation soon turned into a kind of deep sorrow bordering on depression. As I said, the Summer Course was on. The students would have *darshan* twice a day instead of the normal once a day. Salt would be rubbed into my wounds twice a day. I felt Swami was so distant from me. He would even visit the auditorium where the talks were being delivered. Since the auditorium had a limited seating capacity, there would so some students sitting out and I would be a regular. Imagine my plight when Swami went into the auditorium and in between the boys and all I could get was only momentary glances of Him!

And every evening, there would be discourses. That was something that everyone looked forward to. I also enjoyed the discourses because that was the only time when physical proximity did not seem to matter. Two days passed this way and I felt like it was almost a week!

It was the morning of the 29th of May. I was sitting very back and as Swami came for *darshan*, I got tears again. In between the tears, I felt that He was looking at me though He was very far. I wiped my tears and concentrated on Him. I thought that I saw a beautiful smile. That made me so happy. Immediately after the session, I ran to the Warden's office. He was again with some 'big' people and this time, I did not get the VIP treatment! I waited for everyone to leave and then entered his office.

"Sir! Everything is fine!" "What do you mean by that boy?" "Sir! Swami will not throw me out. He is happy with me. He smiled at me..." "Are you sure He smiled at **you**? He could have smiled at anyone else also?" I was in a doubt now. "If you are simply imagining this, then it could end up as disaster for you. You sit in front and show your face and that might be your last *darshan* as a student." I was not ready to take the risk. I again sought his 'protection' and decided to sit back and cool off.

That was not an easy decision. The pressure of sorrow in my heart would never get released by any amount of tears. And so, in the evening too, I was seated somewhere at the back for Swami's discourse. During the course of the discourse, Swami made some statements that almost wrenched my heart. Here is the gist of what He said.

"God does not know the meaning of anger. Can you tell me what anger is? See the rain - it comes as drops of water. At times however, we have hailstones. These cause pain when they strike you but remember that hailstones too are basically water. In the same way, God's anger is also God's love that is packaged in a different manner. God never gets angry."

I have the habit of writing down Swami's discourses even as He speaks. But today, I stopped writing. I was crying within saying, "Swami, you got so angry with me! You say that is your love? Then, I am seeking to get back to you, but I lack courage. I am scared to get thrown out from here and Warden has told me specifically to sit back." The discourse complete, we all moved back to the hostel for dinner and study hours. Soon, it was time to sleep.

Inspiration From Surdas

In the early morning, it was my duty to play music in the PA system of the hostel as everyone finished ablutions and got ready for the day. On the 30th morning, when I played the cassette, the song that played was a composition of Surdas. A brief description of the song is in order here. Sung by the inimitable Anup Jalota, it begins with an introduction:

"Baah Chhudaye Jaat Ho, Nirbal Jaan Ke Mohe. Hriday se Jab Javo Toh, Sabal Mein Jaanu Tohe"

The saint Surdas was blind from birth. He was always lost in the name of Lord Krishna. One day, he falls into a well and calls out to Krishna. A little boy comes up to the well and helps the saint out of the well. Then, as the two are walking together, the saint treats the little boy like a child not knowing that it is his own dear Krishna. And the minute he realises that it is indeed His Lord, Krishna lets go of the hand and runs away. The anguished saint bursts forth into a song. *"Oh Lord! You are thinking me as weak and thus you succeed in freeing yourself from my clasp. But if I am to consider you as really strong, if try to leave my heart where I have bound you."*

Then he goes on to sing the complete song which praises Krishna. Set in the *raag Darbari*, it is such a beautiful experience to hear the song. Though the version here misses the most important opening stanza, it is worth hearing once.

As I heard the song, my heart began to resonate with it. I cried out loud and long to Swami. I said that I was being kept away from Him and that was such a big torture. I also told Him, "You just try as much as you want, you cannot escape from my heart! I hold you dearly there and shall forever hold you that way!" And I cried even more. I was weeping continuously, alone in the audio room. I drifted off into sleep and then Swami came. He came to me in a dream that gave me a hint and a solution to the situation I was in.

The Dream

Anybody who knows the connotation of the 'fruits' of action will easily understand the dream! In the dream, I was seated in the same auditorium that was now hosting the Summer Course. Swami is distributing slices of muskmelon to everyone. Swami was soon about to come into my row of seats to distribute 'fruits'. I then saw that I had some slices of fruit already in my hand. I tried to throw them aside so that I could get the fruits that Swami was giving. I also took out fruit that was in my mouth and tried to throw it away. Swami saw me and said,

"Finish those fruits first. I shall then give you these."

Swami then saw a camera in my hand and frowned. I kept the camera down and quickly ate the fruits that He had referred to. The frown on His face disappeared. I beseeched Him to come near me. Then I told Him,

"Swami I am sorry! You know everything right?"

He simply smiled broadly at me and I felt so happy. "I want to start getting my camera, sitting in front and shooting again."

"No objection", was His reply. He was now sitting beside me on the chair. I asked, "Swami, can I get the camera tomorrow itself?"

He again repeated, "No objection." Then He rose from the chair and left.

Bold Step Taken

I woke up and felt so light in the heart. So, all that had happened was me 'eating the fruits' that I had gathered. Only when those fruits were eaten could my hands be free to receive the fruits He wanted to give. And the dream signified that my fruits had been consumed. I decided that I would take my camera right away. But how was I to get the 'permission slip' necessary to take my camera into the hall? The person in charge for giving permission slips had been specially told about my ban. Not bothering too much about it, I had my bath and found myself whistling joyously too. I got ready and then went to the person in charge for the camera chit. I told him, "Sir, I would like to take my camera for *darshan* today." He simply nodded and signed me a permission slip! Was I amazed!

I went to the first lines along with the 'birthday boys'. Swami came for *darshan*. As He neared me, I was wondering what would happen. Nothing happened - neither a smile, nor a blast. I was happy with that and had some satisfaction welling within me. That satisfaction was only short-lived. The teacher in charge of the audio department called me and asked, "How come you are sitting in the front?"

"Sir! The problem got solved now," I replied. "I asked the Warden. He said nothing about the problem being solved." "Sir! The problem was never between Warden and I. It was between Swami and I and it is solved."

It is little wonder that I was summoned to the Warden's office. "Boy! You were lucky today morning. It is hardly four days since Swami was so upset and you openly flouted what I told you." "Sir! These four days have felt like forty for me! Swami came in my dream and told me that He had no objection. So I will no longer stick to my ban." "Are you sure about this?" "I am very sure Sir. In fact, tomorrow is my duty to be in the audio room. I would like to resume that." "Swami is definitely going to see you there before He goes for *darshan*!" "I know and I want to do it." "You might lose your place in the college..." "Sir! If Swami kicks me out, I shall leave for it is His will. I am not scared anymore."

I walked out of the room. I was very sure that if any 'mishap' were to take place, I would get the 'I-told-you-so' look from Warden. I began to pray to Swami about the next day morning when I would stand right next to the blue carpet on which he would go walking towards the *darshan* hall. I would be all alone there. But I was comforted by two things - one was the dream. The second was the fact that Swami usually walked looking at the ground and carpet in the area that I would be standing. He would look up only after the devotees came in sight. I thought that most probably Swami would pass by me without even noticing me. It was with these thoughts that I welcomed the 3rd of June, 2002.

I arrived early to Swami's residence and set up all the mikes and other audio system. When everything was ready, I took Swami's handkerchief from His chair in our room and kept it in readiness in my pocket. I usually carried a handkerchief for Him always anyway. Then, I took my position by the side of the carpet. I was praying that everything should go on fine. And then, Swami arrived. A hush fell over the entire place.

Swami came walking down the carpet, looking down at the carpet all the while. I was relaxing a bit for things were indeed working out exactly as I had thought. He came just three feet away from me. I could smell His wonderful fragrance even though I held my breath. But then! He stopped right in front of me. My heart skipped a beat. He looked into my eyes. I was inwardly screaming, "Swami! You said that you had no objections and so I came. Do not scold me..."

"Where are the fruits?", He asked.

I was dumbstruck. I immediately remembered my dream and was about to say, "Swami I ate them", but I stopped. I saw far into the background where students stood in readiness with basketfuls of mangoes. I realized that mangoes would be distributed as *prasadam* today. So I said, "Swami the fruits are there." He smiled. He looked at the boys and called one of them. He felt the mangoes and told me, "These should be distributed after the *bhajans.*"

I nodded with an understanding smile and offered the kerchief to Him as His hands had been 'soiled' by the touch of mangoes. He took it, wiped His hands and playfully threw it back at my face. He beamed another smile and walked on. Everything became so clear for me. Once the message becomes clear, the messenger ceases to exist. Anger was simply a messenger here! The Warden and my teacher in-charge, came to me and broadcasted smiles. They said, "Swami is so happy with you." I was again crying!

Chapter 16

Visualising And Materialising The Lord

Being a devotee of Sri Sathya Sai Baba, it will not be an exaggeration to say the 24th of April, 2011, was the saddest day of my life. Swami, whom I consider as my Master, best friend and the light of my life, departed from the physical to the realms of the spiritual. I am sure that it was a shock to so many of His followers and devotees also.

But before you think that this is going to be an outpouring of grief, let me stop. This is more an expression of relief and joy. Why? Let me say this much that there are ways in which we are able to 'see' Him and feel His presence even now. While manifestations and miracles happening depend on His will, there is one powerful technique that we can definitely adopt to open up a communication channel with dear Swami!

Unknowingly, I have used this technique in the past and the result was amazing. It is almost as if Swami can be bound permanently! I shall narrate that experience shortly but the best thing - this technique has been given by Swami Himself!

Even as I think of sharing this, it seems Swami wants to add another experience to the same. In course of an email conversation, my Chemistry teacher, Dr.K.Anil Kumar (*not to be confused with Swami's translator*) shared his experience. It is actually to him that Swami gave the technique. Thus, it is with great joy that I present his experience which is His present to me.

The setting:

Prasanthi Nilayam, Puttaparthi in the summer of 1981 (or maybe 1982)

The situation:

Swami is residing in the room above the interview room in the Prasanthi Mandir itself. *Darshan* is at about 6:30-7:00am while *bhajans* are from 11:00am to 11:30am. Evening *bhajans* are from 5:30pm to 6:00pm. It is the summer vacations and, so, there are very few students. Some students have arrived from the Brindavan campus and Anil Kumar is one among those students.

The Prelude To The Experience

The evening session has just concluded. Swami has moved into the interview room where He will have His few morsels which He calls 'dinner'! The students, like every day, decide to wait till He retires to His room above. Who knows, they may be lucky enough to catch another glimpse of Him. It was a chance that was not to be allowed to slip; after all, it was only the students who had the permission and opportunity to wait thus.

It turns out to be a very memorable day for the students who decided to wait that day. The interview room door opens and out walks Swami. His presence is powerful with His huge mop of hair and flowing robe. There is complete silence till Swami looks at all the students and beckons them to go into the interview room. The silence is shattered by the thundering of footfalls as all the students rush towards the interview room like iron filings towards a powerful magnet. The 'magnet' is the last to move into the interview room. It is a small room, about 6 feet by 11 feet in size and yet it seems to have a magical capacity to accommodate all those that need to be inside!

Once Swami is inside, the room is filled with laughter and merry talk as He starts pulling legs and cracking jokes. Soon, everyone is in a very happy and light mood. The situation is set for sowing some seeds of wisdom. Swami begins to speak on how *bhajans* should be sung,

"Whenever the name of the Lord is sung, dwell on the meaning of the name. The name of the Lord is as powerful as His form. While singing *bhajans*, the head, the heart and the hands must be involved. For instance, take the name - Gopala (one who tends and takes care of the cow - Krishna). The cow, after giving birth to a calf, licks it clean. If a "Go" (cow) can have such love, imagine the love embodied by 'Gopala'. Feel this love as you sing about Gopala. Picture your God and pour out your feelings. They will reach Him."

The session comes to a close too soon. (Any session with Swami seems to come to an end too soon!) Anil Kumar is inspired by what Swami has said and decides to implement it with immediate effect. He starts practicing to feel intensely during *bhajans*, visualizing Swami on a regular basis.

The Student's Experience With Visualization

One of the days, Swami goes out for a drive to supervise a construction site during the *bhajans*. Anil Kumar sang the *bhajans* with visualization which had now become his regular practice. He pictures Swami standing in front of Him and gently swaying to the tune of the *bhajan*. In his mind's eye, he sees the trees gently swaying in the breeze and the birds merrily chirping.

The orange of Swami's robe seems to blend in with the orange of the skies as the sun is setting. Swami's presence fills his whole heart, and thus, his world too. Slowly, tears of joy begin to form and trickle down his cheek. He is lost in the beauty of *darshan* and he realizes the meaning of what Swami had said a few days before. Though Swami is not in the *mandir*, he is not missing Him. And the beautiful experience continues.

One *bhajan* later, he suddenly feels a hush all around. And his beautiful meditation seems to get disturbed. It is almost as if someone by his side is tapping gently to call him. Leaving aside the beautiful image of the swaying Swami, he opens his eyes to determine the source of 'disturbance'. As he opens his eyes, he is in for a blissful surprise. The mental image of Swami, instead of disappearing, gets reinforced as Swami is there, right in front of him! And He is swaying gently, EXACTLY as he is picturing Him. Swami's face is glowing in joy and a gentle smile is dancing on His lips. As Anil Kumar gazes longingly at the form that is the object of his adoration and love, Swami walks up to him. He smiles at him and says, "Inside Swami - outside Swami are ONE." Then He walks away.

I was so thrilled hearing about this. It was such a beautiful blessing from Swami because I wanted to share a very similar experience. This narrative was a bolster for me.

My Experience:

I have constantly pined for physical attention from Swami. It was during my undergraduate days at Brindavan that I came up with this 'visualization' technique, totally by instinct and chance.

What I used to do was this - I would close my eyes and picture myself with Swami. I would speak with Him and also 'make' Him speak to me. I mean, I would put words in His mouth. And since it was Him, the words I would put in His mouth would also be of that nature. In this manner, I would close my eyes and converse with my beloved Lord, my best friend. In due course, my imagination and visualization became so powerful that every day, I would feel as if I had an interaction with Swami. Soon, I stopped pining so much for the 'physical' interactions. I had my 'own, personal Swami' now!

One day, I suddenly had a doubt, "Is this imagination and visualization a hallucination on my part? Am I being spiritual or am I being schizophrenic?" This was a time when Swami, for some reason, was not accepting letters from any student. As I lay down to sleep, I began my conversation with 'my Swami'. I told Him,

"Swami please take my letter tomorrow..." "No! I have been telling that I will not accept letters from students for some time. I cannot take it from you." "Swami! Please. You must take it. It is very important for me because I want to know that you are for real." "Of course I am for real... Why do you doubt?" "I don't know Swami. But please take my letter." "If I take your letter, then others will feel bad. They will get jealous of you." "Swami, I shall sit in a corner. Take my letter in a manner such that nobody sees it. Thus, no one will feel bad or get jealous. I shall also be happy and know that you are for real. I promise I will not tell anyone that you took my letter." "Hmm.. Okay. Let's do that."

I must say that this whole conversation was completely made up in my mind on my own. The next day, something amazing happened. I was in the corner with my letter. Swami indeed came near me. I showed my letter, but He did not accept it. He passed by me and stood next to me, talking to a devotee. I was disappointed and feeling that either Swami had disappointed me or 'my Swami' was not real. As I was coming to terms with what was happening, Swami brought His hands behind Him and held His left wrist with His right hand. And then, it happened!!

He moved His left hand fingers so gently. But via His fingers, He was asking for my letter!! I slowly took my letter near His fingers. In an instant, He took the letter and then moved on. I was dumbstruck. Great joy erupted in my heart. I was almost trembling with excitement and joy. The students by my side were wondering what happened. 'Sadly', I could not tell them anything for that was my promise to 'my Swami'. My heart celebrated for I was sure that 'my Swami' is real. I had found a way of having Him with me always.

Dear reader. Trust me. Go ahead and visualize your Lord. Put in as many details as possible in your visualization. Live it. Re-live it. Enjoy it. Know that it is true. Your own experience is just waiting to happen. It is just round the corner. It is not simply that it is said, *"Mana Eva Manushyanaam Kaaranam Bandha Mokshayoho"* (The mind alone is responsible for one's bondage or liberation). The Vedas declare, *"Antar Bahischa Tat Sarvam Vyapya Narayana Sthitaha"* (in spirit this means - Whether it is the inner world or the outer world, the Lord is ever present.) If I am allowed to use, with slight modification, the famous quote from the Tale of Two Cities by Charles Dickens:

It is the worst of times; it is the best of times. It is the age of foolishness; it is the age of wisdom. It is a season of darkness; it is a season of light. It is the winter of despair, it is the spring of hope. It is a time when everything has changed; it is a time when nothing has changed! The fact that Swami is not with us physically is a great opportunity for each one of us to discover our personal Swami within. And believe me, He is as real as real can be.

Chapter 17

Swami Teaches Me The Difference Between Love And Attachment

Unrequited love has been defined as a love that is not understood and reciprocated by the object of love, which is usually a person. The 'beloved' may be unaware of the 'admirer's' deep affections or may not want to reciprocate even after knowing what the 'admirer' feels. And when it comes to the suffering and pain, it is always the case of grass being greener on the other side. The 'admirer' feels that life is so simple for the 'admired' wishing that there is someone to pine for him/her in a similar manner. The 'admired' feels that the 'admirer' is simply complicating life, gets embarrassed and wonders why he/she is being stalked.

And there are broken hearts, pieces of which lie scattered along many life-journeys.

It is not as if unrequited love happens only in romantic relationships. Platonic friendships, which are based on strong, non-romantic attachment too provide a fertile soil for such love. In these cases, a friend, an acquaintance or a colleague becomes the object of unrequited love. So well-known are cases of unrequited love that poems, songs, books and movies have been made on such themes. Almost everyone has faced this either as an 'admirer' or as an 'admired' at some point of time of their lives. While some may whine saying that one-way love is at least better than having a completely dry life, those that have been part of the one-way love feel that it is best to be away from such things rather than have the heart broken.

So, what is this true love? Is it a myth? When love is supposed to elicit love, why does it not seem to be doing so? And when love is not returned, why does the person not just understand and go away? All these questions arise like a sandstorm in the heart, breaking it into tiny pieces in the fury of its gusto. The greatest adventure and experience in my life has been in experiencing true love and thus understanding some of its facets. Before I embark on sharing these insights, I wish to make that task easy by sharing my own little story on unrequited love and a dozen heart-breaks.

The Story Of A Dozen Friendships - And A Dozen Heartbreaks

The story begins from my school days. I was a person who would get attached to people very fast. If anybody was nice to me and shared their affections with me, I would grow very fond of them. This trait of mine was nourished and nurtured by many friendships that I made. I was fiercely possessive about my friends and very loyal to them too. And I had many circles of friendship, with a select few in the innermost one - for whom I would be ready to do anything! Though a friend would enter my life from the outermost circle, with a little understanding, empathy, affection and kindness, he/she would be able to work the way through to the inner circles.

I have made use of the past tense in my narrative because today, I am not like that. I still love people with great intensity but I do not get attached to them as I used to. The happenings during my 2nd year undergrad, in the academic year 2001-2002 have been important in shaping me in this manner. I was a student of the Brindavan campus of the Sri Sathya Sai Institute of Higher Learning.

I shall not go into the minute details of my unrequited love for I wish to present the answers. The pains of unrequited love that I went through were the same - my 'best-friends' not coming up to my expectations, me not getting in return what I was giving out liberally to my friends, my friends not even knowing that they were paining me and, to top all of that, some of them even wondering why I was acting so 'crazy'.

During these days, the worst part of my days were the nights. The schedule for the students at the Institute has been set so wonderfully by Swami that if it is followed sincerely, it does not allow any student time for distractions. It keeps him completely immersed in academics, extra-curricular activities, prayers, social service and integrated personality development that it is tribute to the monkey mind that one is able to find time for distractions!

And my mind found this 'devil's workshop' timing from 9:30 pm to 10:00 pm. The dinner and study hours would be complete by 9:30 pm and it was lights-out at 10:10 pm. Those 40 minutes, I would 'visit' my friends in their rooms, talk and interact with them. I thought of these minutes as a very happy time. But it was also the seedbed for growing expectations. I would visit a sick friend and tend to him for long. But I would expect the same treatment when I was sick, but that would not happen. I would work extra hard to make special cards for my friends' birthdays, but I did not receive such special cards from them! (You get the idea right?)

So, as I would sleep at night, I would cry over why these friends were not responding to the love and affection in my heart. Little did I know then that intertwined along with the purity of my love were the dreadful strings of attachment also.

The Trip To Puttaparthi - A Hope Beckons

I decided to seek Swami's help out of this. There were a hundred other things in my life which He had helped solve and I was sure that He would help me out with this too. We would be soon visiting Puttaparthi for the Sports Meet on January 11th, 2002. I wrote a letter to Swami about how each and every friend of mine had failed me and how desperately I wanted His help, strength and understanding from within, to deal with this. I cried bitter tears as I wrote that letter and I asked Swami as to why love was never appreciated in the world. (The mind goes into such foolish assumptions very quickly. It makes one feel that one is being very noble in love. It makes attachment, infatuation and the burden of expectations to be confused as love.)

By January 5th we were at Prasanthi Nilayam, Puttaparthi. I carried my letter with me for daily darshans whenever I could. I never got a chance to give the letter to Swami. And even at Puttaparthi, my pain from unrequited 'love' continued. For instance, I would tell a friend of mine that I would be joining him for dinner at the canteen and I so I wait for him to return from Sports practice. But when he returns, he has already had his dinner and he says,

"Gosh I forgot. Am sorry."

Thats all! He does not even know that I have not yet had my dinner. And if I state that, I will be accused of being clingy. (Let me be honest - I was clingy! And stupid too. And I mistook that to be love and friendship.)

Amidst all this, I get no solace from Swami. No letter-acceptance, no smile, no pat on the head and no consoling words. The Sports meet concluded on 11th and the 14th was the prize distribution. I wrote a fresh letter because I was sure that when I went on stage to pick up the winners' shield for the Institute Debate, I would get a chance to hand over the letter to him. Frankly speaking, I was most eager about being able to give this letter and do away with a terrible problem in my life - more than about receiving a shield from Him. I wanted a 'shield' of another kind.

But on the 14th of January, 2002, as I went up to him with my fellow-participant to take the shield, I did not even get a look of recognition. Of course, Swami presented us the shield and posed with us for a photograph. But he did not pat me on my back nor take my letter. Nor did He give me a reassuring smile. To add pain to this, he patted the other's shoulder! I returned to my place with great sorrow in my heart – a sorrow that I could share with none for none would understand, even Swami (or so I thought).

I was a prize-winner no doubt, but the prize I sought was a shield of a different nature.

Divine Love And Light

The next day we started back towards our campus in Brindavan, Bengaluru. I was in a state of complete sadness. The feeling of being a 'victim' of unrequited love was enhanced by Swami's apparent indifference to what I was going through. I wondered as to when I would get the next chance to convey to Him what I felt and give Him my letter. The next trip for Shivaratri was at least more than a month away.

In the meanwhile, we reached our destination and it was with a certain amount of dread that I faced the prospect of another night without a solution. My damned attachment was so strong that I could not even restrain myself from going and interacting with my friends. I decided that this night I would not go anywhere. I would simply go to bed.

"But what if some friend comes to me and talks to me?", I thought. I again prayed to Swami to help me love the way He loves. And in an instant, a magical and totally unexpected thing happened.

I was summoned to the warden's office or 'the den' as we used to call it. Sri.B.N.Narasimhamoorty was the warden, a man who commanded great awe and respect. I entered the office and the first statement he told me, simply swept me off my feet,

"Swami wants you to sleep every night in His residence, Trayee Brindavan. This means you will have to go in by 8:00pm and be all by yourself till next day morning 5:00am. Are you ready?"

What was I to say?

He continued,

"Swami said that some students should sleep in Trayee Brindavan for security. He personally picked the boys and you are one among them. Get your bedding and shift to Trayee Brindavan."

This was a boon from the highest heavens. And adding to that boon was the next statement,

"You will continue to sleep there even when Swami is in Brindavan."

Sleeping one floor below Swami's bedroom! What a boon!

Seeking God's Love Alone Is The Solution

As I lay on the bed looking at the balcony from which Swami gives darshan after every Trayee session, I was simply lost. My mind was blank and heart was rejoicing. In a single moment, Swami had solved my 'friendship' problems! I was not connected to Him so strongly that the other attachments felt weak and loose.

Today, when I look back to that special 'first night', so much clarity evolves. Unrequited love is nothing but attachment, desire and, at times, infatuation or a combination of all of these. Love is always blissful. Love is divine. And Love is always one for it always comes from God alone.

I realized that throughout my life, whenever I 'liked' a person or 'loved' a person, it was because of some nice feelings and thoughts that the person evoked in me. It was because he/she gave me love and affection of some kind. What I failed to see was that this love was God's love coming to me through a particular person. Instead of getting attached to the love, I got attached to the person.

What do I mean? When I was sick, I was looking forward for my 'special friends' to come and tend for me, all the while neglecting my roomies and other classmates who came to be with me. So lost was I searching for expressions of love in a few that I missed the very same expressions from many others! How many times have I missed God's love because it comes in a form that I am not expecting?

Swami has exhorted a thousand times that His love for me is always with me, in me, above me, below me and around me. He says that I will never be away from His love. But I miss it all the while because I am looking for it only in a few forms! Oh! What a mistake it is to give importance to the conduits of love rather than love? It is like licking with parched tongues on a dry pipe allowing water to gently gurgle out of another pipe nearby. Is the water more important or the pipe?

And thus, the difference between infatuation and love boils down to what I seek. When I seek love, for it is my default mode to do so, it is fine. But when I seek the form, the body or the object through which I feel I can experience love, it becomes infatuation. One is then unable to let go of that object of love even if loves ceases to flow from it! The irony is that there is always an abundance of love for any seeker of love. One just has to make sure that it is love that one is seeking and not its container.

Finally, I understand what Swami means by saying the heart is not musical chairs but a single-seater sofa. It has place only for one. And that 'one' should be God's love because that is all there is in the universe. My heart is a container that should not hold pipes but the water. Who cares from which pipe the water flows? And my God is the only reservoir of water.

I prayed and I continue to make that prayer even today,

"Swami, let my love for you and thirst for your love grow stronger each passing moment."

If I seat many on a single-seat sofa and it breaks, is it not natural? Let me seat only ONE and let that be my God! For, God is love and love is God.

Chapter 18

God Sees The Truth But Waits...

The Amazing Krishna Janmashtami Experience...

In a collection of short stories by the greatest writers in the world, I came across a story by Leo Tolstoy with the title, "God sees the Truth but waits...". It was a very powerful read and it showed how God allows seemingly 'bad' things to happen so that ultimately, the individual benefits the maximum. The story depicted the difference between worldly love and divine love. Worldly love cares only about the joys of the body and the mind. Divine love is ready to sacrifice the body and the mind at the altar of the soul! The story is a reminder that whatever happens in life is always good for us. And that is the true meaning of surrender as Swami revealed so beautifully to a student. It brings to my mind Swami's saying, "What you meet in life is destiny, how you meet it is self-effort." It also brings to my mind an episode and an event that reassured me about Swami's all-knowing nature. He sees everything. He knows everything. And yet, He waits...

Let me take you back to the year 2004. I was studying as a 2nd year Post Graduate in Chemistry at the Swami's Institute. It was that golden period of my student days when Swami took a lot of interest in student programmes. He encouraged us to put up programmes in His Divine presence. In fact, on one occasion, when the Warden requested Swami to come and sit outside between the *darshan* and *bhajan* sessions, Swami said, "Why should I? There is no programme today!" We had no idea then that this kind of 'programming' would become the precursor to a plethora of programmes by the different State and International Sathya Sai Organizations later. However, we were happy to be part of Swami's plan. In fact, seeing so many programmes that were being demanded by Swami of the students, the seniors in the organization thought of providing 'relief' by passing a resolution that different groups would that visited Prashanti should also have a Cultural Programme ready for presentation. Today, when I look back at those days, I get goose bumps realising how Swami was preparing a new mode of chances for devotees from the world over – through songs, dramas and other programmes in His presence.

The 'Programmer's Dilemma'...

Getting back to the story, it was the first day in the month of September, 2004. September 6th was Krishna Janmashtami and I got an idea that we should put up a programme in Swami's presence for that occasion. We were the senior most class in the hostel and we had been given the privilege of proposing programmes at short notice. However, the idea was not given an enthusiastic reception. Though there were a few who backed the idea and were enthusiastic like me, most of the 'necessary individuals' did not warm up to the idea. Their reasons were:

1. We had already put up three programmes in the past month and there was a kind of 'saturation'!

2. Just because Swami was giving us chances, it did not mean that we should put up programmes in such a hurry.

3. The monthly tests were round the corner and all had to get busy studying. I could see meaning in the reasoning, but somehow, my reasoning did not make sense to them. My reasoning was:

1. Swami is giving chances and we should grab them with both hands.

2. If we take care of our intention and keep prayers going, Swami will take care of the programme.

However, there were about 4-5 good speakers in the class who agreed with my idea and we decided that we would go ahead with the programme. We decided that the format would be two comperes hosting the programme with a few songs and dances interspersed in between. Since there were six of us, we divided ourselves into 3 compere-pairs. We requested the students from the higher secondary school to prepare a couple of dances. We requested the *bhajan* group to prepare some songs. There is a reason why am narrating all these details and I request the reader's indulgence for a while more.

The six of us met up to decide what should be the theme of the programme and it was a combined inspiration that we should re-live the story of lord Krishna in a different perspective. For instance, there is the episode of Vasudeva's chains dropping away when baby Krishna was born. The prison doors opened and the father got the chance to take the child safely away to Gokul, away from the wrath of the demon Kamsa. On his return to the prisons, the gates got locked again and his shackles bound him. We interpreted this as once you 'pick' up God, you are 'set free' and when you 'put down' God, you are 'bound and shackled." The entire programme was a creative interpretation like this. We had to ensure the programme quality with our content for we had nothing on the 'presentation' front with all our 'class' performers backing out of the programme. In fact, I remember calling one of my friends, Raju, on the intercom phone from my room and shedding tears, "Why are we not getting any support for this programme? Swami definitely sees what the 'anti-programmers' are feeling. But does He not see what our intentions and feelings are?"

Raju reassured me, "Don't worry. Our motives and feelings are pure. Swami will support us. Let us go and read all of Swami's discourses on Krishnashtami and we will get more ideas on the content."

We approached the Warden and told him that we would be ready with a programme for Krishnashtami. He was happy (and was unaware of all that we were going through) and himself told a wonderful experience.

When he was a student, Swami had visited the hostel on a Krishna Janmashtami day. He spoke only about the Krishna avatar. While narrating how Lord Krishna would go with his cowherd friends, the gopalas, for grazing cows, Swami said, "Krishna would tie a cloth around his head when he was with the cows." Swami then asked for a piece of cloth. The Warden, a student then, ran to his room and fetched his towel. Swami took it from him and to the great joy and wonder of all the students present there, tied it around His head, the way Krishna would! Ah! That was pure delight and Swami too was beaming a smile. Listening to Warden's narrative made us feel better and we slept well that night.

Divine Assistance...

The next day, we headed off to the library, not for studies but to research all of Swami's Krishnashtami discourses. I randomly picked a volume of Sathya Sai Speaks and searched for the Krishnashtami discourse. Immediately, goose bumps erupted on my skin. The discourse was dated September 6th, 1977, the same day when Krishnashtami was on this year too. (The exact day of Krishnashtami varies from year to year since it is decided according to the lunar calendar.)

The goose bumps only grew in size when I read the contents of that discourse. Swami had spoken about the significance of the Krishna avatar and had given the exact same interpretation for the chains falling off as we had thought of the previous day! We hungrily devoured that discourse and gathered more of the content. Even the statement that we would browse through His discourses which Raju had offered reassuringly to me seemed part of His Masterplan. Imagine the thrill we felt when we also discovered the fact that it was during that same discourse in the Brindavan hostel that Swami had tied a towel to His head!

We were sure that this was Swami's way of telling us that He backed us. The six of us prepared with great enthusiasm and joy. But the question still remained – how were we to make a good presentation or programme only with six speakers. There had to be good dances, songs, skits and other such depictions too for a complete programme. We left that worry completely to Swami, who, we were sure by now, was watching over us.

The next couple of days saw us prepare in all thoroughness, but at the end of it, the only programme we had ready were six excellent speeches based on what Swami had said. We also came to know that Swami would be delivering His divine discourse on the Krishnashtami morning, i.e. the 6th of September, 2004 morning.

Suddenly, our programme seemed to make no meaning at all! If Bhagawan was to deliver His discourse, it naturally meant that there would be no other programme that morning. We went to the Warden for his opinion. He told us to be prepared and dressed in our colourful costumes all the same. He said that Swami's will would prevail and that was something we already knew! And so, at the break of dawn on 6th September, I dressed up in a golden-chrome *kurta*. The others too wore their grand dresses. With a prayer on our lips, we set out to the *mandir*. What happened that morning, simply took our breath away and I realized how God always sees the Truth, though He waits!

Krishnashtami Morning

After a lot of effort, which involved our physical, mental, emotional and spiritual strength, we had reached some level of preparedness for the programme. All of us assembled in the Sai Kulwant hall by 6:45am. It was 7:15 am when the golf-cart in which Swami used to arrive for *darshan* was seen entering the hall at the ladies' side of the hall. A gasp of wonder and joy rippled across the hall as everyone realised that Swami was in the beautiful *Pitambara* (yellow robe)!

He took a complete *darshan* round and arrived on the stage. It was as if Swami too was excited about the occasion and had dressed especially for it. We, (our 'programming' group) were seated in the front. We had not told our Warden that our programme predominantly consisted of comperes talking. As far as he was concerned, we had prepared a programme and the success of the previous ten or so programmes had built up his confidence in our word. I felt that all that would change shortly.

Swami called the Vice-Chancellor of the Institute, Sri.S.V.Giri. He enquired as to what programme was there for the day. The Vice-Chancellor had great confidence in the Warden's word and this confidence too was built on the successful conduct of the previous ten or so programmes by students. He confidently told Swami that the senior-most students of the Institute would be putting up a presentation. Swami's face immediately lit up in joy and pride. It was as if He was waiting for this moment when His students would put up the programme.

And now, I come to the sequence of events that unfolded beyond the imagination of any of us. To start with, Swami asked the Vice-Chancellor as to who would be putting up the programme. The Vice-Chancellor looked towards us and in a trice, two of us rushed to the stage. Swami looked at us and asked what the programme was about. In a hurry, we tried to give a gist of all the talks. While doing so, we went through the names of all the six students who were compering and Swami asked for them to come on the stage, one by one.

Within a few minutes, all the six of us were on stage, surrounding Swami's chair. Swami told all of us to sit down. Then He called the Vice-Chancellor and told him to announce the morning programme. The mike and lectern were brought on the dais and the Vice-Chancellor made a public announcement of how the senior students from the Institute would be putting up a 'variety' programme. Once that was done, Swami sent him back to his seat. He now looked at me and told me to start the programme. I indicated

to the other boys on the stage that we should move down and get
things organized.

The six of us comperes were made to sit around His sofa.
We had no idea of what was going to happen.

Programmes those days used to be held by us in a narrow
corridor that existed between Swami and the students. We thus called
these presentations as 'street plays'. More than the costumes and
make-up, our emphasis was always on the content - Swami's
message.

But even as the others got up, Swami told them all to sit. He
told me to proceed. As I mentioned earlier, we had prepared to do
the programme as compere-pairs. And so, I looked at my compering-
partner. He was looking deep into Swami's eyes and drinking in His
darshan. There was no way I could catch his eye. I thought that it
would be best to go to the 'corridor' and start the programme. That
would make him realise that he too had to come down to do the
compering act. With this in mind, as I began to move down the
stage, Swami called me. He pointed to the mike on stage. He said,
"Go there and speak."

I was totally confused. What was I to do? It struck me that maybe Swami wanted me to elaborately introduce the programme. None of the programmes we had done till now had been given an introduction this way. I was thinking, "Swami do not make too much out of this! We do not have such a programme backing up all this introductory grandeur!"

I went to the mike. I was wondering what to speak. I had my lines ready but they were meant for the programme. I quickly recollected some of the material that we had collected for the programme but were not using it. Combining that with some of my compering matter, I gave a brief talk for about five minutes talking about the two avatars - Krishna and Sai. Having done that, I went to Swami and asked whether we could begin the programme.

Swami told me to sit at His feet. He looked at Raju who was by my side and told him to go and speak in the mike. I understood. I whispered to Raju, "Introduce the programme in Telugu." He went to the lectern and spoke for about five minutes in Telugu on what

I delivered all the 'non-programme' lines in my extempore talk that day.

we planned to put up in the programme. Once he finished and returned, Swami asked him also to sit by His chair. He asked the third student to go and speak. By now, I was totally lost as to what Swami's plan was. I just stopped thinking. This student, Jagannathan by name, went to the mike and began to speak out all his prepared content. But he too kept it short - five minutes. In those five minutes, however, he sang a song which the *gopikas* (cowherdesses) used to sing about one devoted *gopika* by name Suguna. Swami thoroughly enjoyed the song.

Then, Swami told the fourth student to speak! By now, I had just stopped thinking and was just witnessing. It is often said that God is simply a witness to all that man does. I feel it is the other way round. God is the only doer and all of us are simply witnesses! One by one, Swami had made all the six of us speak and more than half an hour had elapsed. Once the last student had spoken, Swami smiled and said, "Programme over." Oh my God!!!! He knew that we had no programme ready. He knew that we had all put in efforts. He knew that we would make laughing stock of ourselves had we put up the programme. He knew that our intentions and motives for making the programme were noble. So, He simply conjured up a new 'programme' and made us all 'heroes'! Many times, we do not realise that God makes us work for a result that we never even think of. This brings to my mind the most inspiring and thrilling PUSH story that was mentioned in the 11th chapter of this book.

Swami then stood up and delivered His divine discourse during which He manifested a chain made of 108 gold coins. The six of us were blessed to be sitting around Him during that entire discourse. And guess what that beautiful discourse was about - how the Lord accepts only a pure heart!

Third-person Account

The reports for that day in the different websites were as follows:

After a few minutes, Bhagawan asked the Vice-chancellor to introduce the programme. The VC spoke for a few minutes and asked the boys to commence their presentation. However, instead of the Music Programme, Swami asked each of these boys to give a short talk to the audience. One by one, all the boys took their position in front of the podium and gathering from the material they were to use as part of their presentation and adding few spontaneous remarks and instances, each one got through with an inspiring and interesting talk.

They had no idea of what all had happened. God sees the Truth but waits! He waits for the perfect time and perfect place to bestow the perfect boon. Let me end this narrative with what Swami told the students during that memorable discourse in the Brindavan hostel:

"You have here a picture of Sai standing on a lotus. (That was the picture in the altar there.) Sai Krishna will install Himself in the lotus of your heart. He will ever be with you as guard and guide, and will shower grace on you. He will be the mother, father, preceptor and your nearest kinsman. He will be your all. That is a promise."

6th September, 1977

Chapter 19

Humility: The Hallmark Of A Devotee - My Ego-crushing Experience

"It was pride that changed angels into devils; it is humility that makes men as angels."

- Saint Augustine

"Pride makes us artificial and humility makes us real."

- Thomas Merton

"Love lives by giving and forgiving; Self lives by getting and forgetting."

- Bhagawan Sri Sathya Sai Baba

"Early in life I had to choose between honest arrogance and hypocritical humility. I chose the former and have seen no reason to change."

- Frank Lloyd Right

The subject of humility is so expansive and has so many facets to it. This article is definitely not going to be a treatise on humility for I cannot claim much knowledge or association with it. However, what I definitely know is the power of a hooded 'cobra' known as the ego. I have seen how it enters me in such a subtle and camouflaged manner and, just like in the beginning of alcohol-drinking or smoking, makes me feel good about myself. I indulge in it till it becomes an addiction - one that eventually kills! There have been many occasions when my dear Master and Best-Friend has lovingly taught me to be humble. There have been occasions when He has taught me the same as a 'slap on the face' - a strong wake-up call that is often necessary when one does not seem to change with loving words.

Today, there is some understanding in me about humility. But before I share that, it would be unfair if I do not share the experience of one such 'slap on the face' which I was dealt at the Divine hands. For, I know that the reader comes to read the Divine story and not my interpretation of it! It is only the readers' love for Swami that they indulge me and my 'wisdom sharing'!

"Will Anyone Speak Today?"

It was during the academic year 2004-05 and I was a student of Second year MSc (Chemistry). During those years (as in the previous years too), Swami would surprise all of us students with the question, "Is anyone ready to speak today?" This was a great chance and responsibility at the same time. To stand beside Swami, share the dais with Him and speak to the thousands that had gathered in the Sai Kulwant Hall was also a great challenge. There have

I prided myself in my ability to churn out speeches in a row, whenever Swami wished.

been many occasions when Swami has rewarded the student who bravely ventured to accept the chance with a ring or chain that He created with a wave of His palm. There have also been many occasions when students have become overnight heroes by simply rising up to the challenge that an extempore speech in His presence presents.

Seeing all this from a very external and superficial point of view, I had some very wrong notions and concepts. This, in part was because I was desperate to 'get into form' or interact with Swami in some way or the other. While there is nothing wrong in that desire, at times the eagerness to fulfil takes one along paths that are best avoided. I took one path like this though I started off with good intentions.

I had armed myself with a well-prepared talk, just in case Swami asked for any speakers during the *mandir* session. One day, it happened. Swami asked the Warden, Sri Shiva Shankar Sai, whether there were any speakers from among the students. I put up my hand and got the call to the dais. I saw that I was the only one to put up my hand. I felt a surge of happiness within me because I seemed to be the only one who was willing to be brave enough to fulfil Swami's desire! There, ego had sneaked in! The talk went on fine. There was applause in the end and I felt so happy that I could stand a few feet away from my Lord, delivering a talk. Needless to say, I was a hero in the hostel and I enjoyed every bit of the adulation I received. So lost was I in my happiness that it was being fuelled by ego and pride, that I failed to notice the fact that Swami did not seem too pleased at the end of my talk.

The Second Chance - A Failure Again

Immediately, after that talk, I prepared another talk. I wanted to be ready whenever Swami asked. The efforts were good, but the motivation was not all that pure. Very soon, a second chance arrived. Swami asked whether there were any students ready to speak and I was the only one to raise my hand immediately and head to the dais. However, even as I neared Swami to take *namaskar*, I heard Him ask the Warden, "Aren't there any other boys in the hostel? This boy keeps coming over and over again."

That statement hurt me (my ego actually). In a moment, thoughts created a whirlpool in my head. "Swami! I am coming here and saving Your students from disgrace. If I do not step up, there will be none ready to speak - and speak well at that! Instead of complimenting me and giving me a pat on the back, you ask such a question to the Warden?" I knelt before Swami and asked Him, "Swami, do you want me to speak or not?" "Go... go... Go and speak," was the simple and terse reply. There seemed to be some sort of an irritation in His voice.

As I stood at the lectern to speak, I found it so difficult. The cancerous growth, my ego, was hurting and I felt that I was hurting. I felt that Swami was not recognising my efforts when the truth was that I was being blind to my ego that had crept in and grown like a

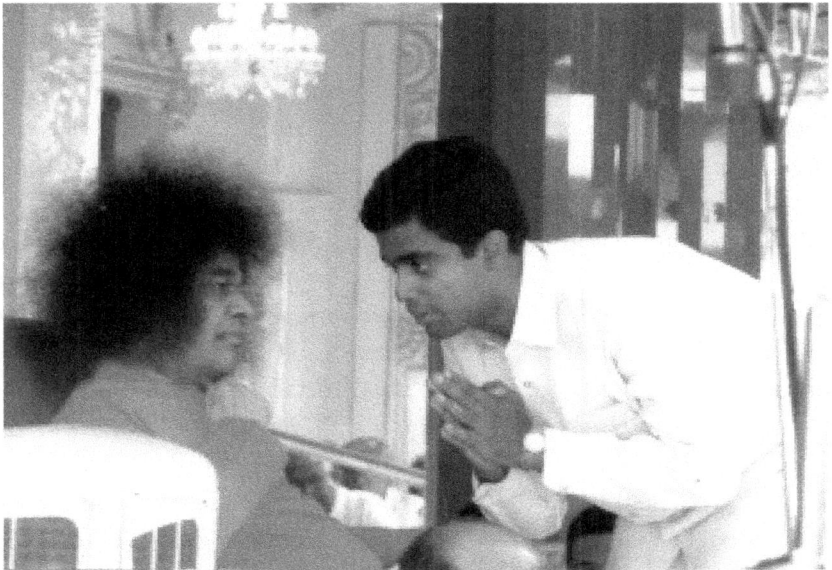

The ego cuts the conversation between man and God.

monster. I completed the speech and returned to my place. The talk
was received well but Swami did not seem all that happy. And I
noticed it this time. I made a resolve, "Swami! Never again will I
raise my hand when you ask for speakers. Then you will realize
what an important job I am doing for you."

The Third Chance - My Refusal

Very soon, came the day when my eyes were opened to what
had been actually happening inside me. It was a day when my ego
was exposed. It started off with Swami asking, "Is anyone ready to
speak today?"

Though I had a speech prepared mentally, I did not raise my
hand. I was determined to make Swami 'realize His fault'. I looked
around. I saw that nobody else was raising a hand. I smiled within
myself and thought that in case nobody lifted their hand for a few
more moments, I would raise mine. I did not want to 'punish' Swami
too much!

Suddenly, one other student raised his hand. I saw him and
was shocked too. I had never heard him in public. I knew that he
had no experience in public speaking. I wondered as to how he was
ever going to speak. As I expected, the speech turned out to be a
poor one. The ego within rejoiced because this boy's 'bad speech'
seemed to add more to the importance of my contribution as a
speaker. As the boy concluded his six-minute speech, there was a
muffled applause. That applause was more like charity from the
audience, I felt. But then, something shocking happened. Swami
gave a broad smile and clapped hard. Instantly, the whole hall was
transformed into a madly applauding gathering of thousands! Swami
blessed the boy profusely and asked for another speaker. It was like
rewind and play for me as another first-timer walked to the dais,
delivered what I considered as a 'sub-standard' talk and received
thunderous applause from the audience, courtesy of Swami's
appreciation!

This happened not twice or thrice but five times as five students spoke in a span of half an hour! At the end of that session came the ultimate salt (and even pepper) to my ego wounds. Swami called the Warden and said, "Speeches should be like this. All boys spoke well!"

Lessons Galore

Today, when I look back at the whole episode, I realise how foolish and blind I was. It is so important to be on God's side for the world always is happy when God is happy. Instead, if God is unhappy, even the greatest skills, talents and performances are of no use. And HUMILITY is what pleases the Lord. Humility does not mean self-deprecation. Nor does it indicate a low self-esteem. It only means that one is not involved in the self but involved in the Self! For, the same Self pervades all beings - call it God, Atma, Spirit or Energy. Humility lies in not being selfish but becoming Self-ish, like the Self! I do not think that my lessons in humility are done. I am still learning and hope to do so always. For, in matters of lessons in humility, when I think that I have learned, I have lost all that I learned!

It was a few months after this that one of the defining experiences of my life chronicled in the article, "When God teaches you to walk: Footprints in the sand", occurred.

Chapter 20

When God Teaches You To Walk - Footprints In The Sand

The Setting For The Unforgettable Experience

Early into my teens, I had read the famous story of the footprints in the sand. For those who are not familiar with it, let me recall it briefly. A person dreams about his life as a walk with God on a beach. He therefore notices two sets of footprints in the sand. But to his dismay, he sees only one set of footprints in those parts of the beach which represent the most difficult times in his life.

He asks God, "Why did you abandon me when I needed you the most?"

God replies lovingly, "Child! Those times when you see only one set of footprints are actually the times when I carried you!"

In spite of knowing this story, there were times when I was convinced that I was absolutely alone in life. And I felt that the single set of footprints were definitely not of His lotus feet, but of my own weary soles! I prayed to God,

"Swami, I just do not believe that you are carrying me now for I feel so much pain and depression. Is that how one feels when one is carried?"

This happened many times but like the proverbial passing clouds, everything would soon clear and days got brighter. But then came the mammoth cloud, so huge that I felt this time the clouds were there to stay. It is about that climactic period I was made to weather that I want to tell about - more so because this episode seasoned my life with the realisation of Swami's omnipresence and love for me.

The Beginning Of A Lifetime Seasoning...

Sorrows And Disappointments Galore...

Since I loved to do public speaking and was involved in dramatics, I was often part of every programme that was being put up in front of Swami. I was doing well on the academic front and I was quite popular among my friends in the hostel. I did fairly well in games and was the shuttle badminton champion for that year. Why I am telling all this is just to show that one may seem to have everything in life and still be unhappy. My God! Why was I unhappy?

When I think back today, I cannot put a finger on the exact reason but I used to be very sad most of the times. And the major reason for this was my attachment to friends. What do I mean by that? Well, I thought that I was a fast friend to quite a few people. I went out of my way to help them and make them feel special. That was fine. The problem came when I expected them to treat me in the same way - that too in a manner I was expecting them to! And this expectation was very strong. As a result, I used to feel very bad.

At this time, I decided that since God was my only true friend, I would look to Him for solace and support. I wanted to extend my arm of unconditional friendship to Him and wanted Him to extend His. I began to curb all my feelings and interactions with friends as much as possible and confided everything to Sai, the resident of my heart - my joys and sorrows, my successes and defeats. This came as a relief but still the disappointments and hurts from my friends continued.

(Today I know that it is not anyone's fault. The nature of the world is thus and the nature of the mind is thus! Nobody will ever understand me fully! How can they when they do not read my mind?)

Life went on this way and I am sure many of my friends wondered what on earth was I sad about. I myself had no answer. The sadness was deep within and it was a kind of dissatisfaction in the search for some permanence. Meanwhile in the *mandir*, speeches, songs and programmes by the students were on regularly. I even got two chances to speak in Swami's presence. They were like bright spots in the dark skies but I was in search of my Sun - Swami as my dearest friend. One day, Swami asked in the *mandir*,

"Are there any boys who wish to speak?"

I raised my hand and Warden told Swami that I was prepared. When I went ahead to take his blessings, I overheard Him ask the Warden,

"Aren't there any other boys? This boy alone speaks always!"

That made me feel very bad. I was hurt. I gave my speech that day but resolved never to raise my hand to speak in His presence. I told my Swami in the heart, "This is the last time I'll raise my hand. I extended my hand in friendship to you and you do not want me to speak in your presence!"

A childish reaction indeed, but that was what I felt then.

I Become The Bleeding Frog In My Opinion

Once, a frog was injured when Lord Rama placed his bow on the ground. Seeing the bleeding frog, when the Lord asked, "Why did you not cry out for help?" the frog replied, "Lord! Every time I am hurt, I call out your name. Now when you place your bow on me, whom should I call out to?" I felt exactly like that frog! And so the days got lonelier and more miserable. I now did not have any more conversations with my heart-resident Swami. Nor did I talk intimately to any of my friends. I felt that my life was so meaningless and all my achievements were nought as I had no happiness. And then came the Sports Meet 2005.

I enrolled in the carabining event and it was to be that sort of an item that is considered the "icing on the cake". But as I said, the clouds began to thicken. The trainer cum coach who was from Singapore somehow got the impression that though I was skilful in carabining, I was not disciplined enough. So he disqualified me from performing in front of Swami on the D day! I was devastated but I decided not to quit and put up a brave face. I used to go daily for the practices telling myself, "Swami is trying to make me feel miserable. I won't give Him victory!" Poor Swami got the blame for my indiscipline.

My teacher in charge however, melted at my misfortune and told me, "Don't worry! When Swami comes to see the practice sessions, I will ensure that you do carabining in His presence."

Now that was something I looked forward to. Days passed and one day I had a bout of severe diarrhoea. My teacher in charge excused me from practice and so, instead of staying in the ground, I went to *mandir* for darshan. The clouds became their thickest when Swami decided to go to the grounds that same day to watch the carabining practice. With tears streaming down my cheeks I returned to the ground and saw Swami enjoy the whole event as the boys practiced. And when He left in the car, He turned His face away exactly at the point when I came in front of his window. I stood devastated! I went back crying to the hostel and told Swami,

"You never give me anything. You have planned my life in such a way that I always get pain . I have always tried to put in my efforts and come up and you have always put me down. And you have given me nothing."

The Bandage? Or Another Poke?

Fast forward to January 11th when the Sports meet went on very well and it was acclaimed that the carabining event was the best! It added the salt from my sweat and tears at sitting in the sidelines to my deep emotional wounds. Now fast forward to the night of January 13th. The Warden asked me whether I would be ready to speak in front of Swami the next day, i.e. Sankranthi and the prize distribution. I was shocked and I asked, "Sir, did Swami ask for me?" He said, "No. tomorrow the Vice-Chancellor and Principal will be speaking. In case Swami asks for student speakers, your name will be suggested along with Raju and Jagdish."

Now Raju was Swami's favourite speaker and when he spoke Telugu, it was as if Mother Saraswati (the Goddess of Learning) sat on his tongue. The same was the story with Jagdish when it came to Hindi. Having considered this along with the "fact" that Swami was least interested in me, I went to bed without preparing anything at all.

The Turning Point

The next morning, I went to the *mandir* without a proper shave or a bath! I cannot believe it now, but that's how depressed I was. On being scolded by a teacher, I went to a nearby saloon to get my stubble shaved and returned to *mandir*. Swami arrived and after the Principal of the Brindavan campus had made his welcome speech, the Vice-Chancellor, Sri.S.V.Giri began his speech. In sharp contrast to my pathetic state, Raju and Jagdish were dressed like princes! As

I sat like a corpse, Swami suddenly intervened in Giri Sir's speech and called him. Sri Giri heard what Swami had to say and returned to the lectern and began, "Bhagawan has blessed two students to speak to us today..." "Raju and Jagdish surely..." I thought. "The first is Ms.Tina Thomas from the Anantapur campus." He went about introducing her. "The second will be one of these two," I thought.

"The second is Aravind Balasubramanya." I was shocked. I was so absolutely unprepared. And I had not even submitted my bio-data to Sri Giri. So he introduced me as "...the boy who did carabining." "What a joke!" I thought but I had to speak!

I tried to glean tidbits from Raju and Jagdish as they had prepared well for their talks. But my predecessor was very strict in her adherence to time. I had barely begun collecting thoughts when she concluded to a rousing applause. I picked a rose and a lot of courage and moved to Swami. I told Him, "Swami please, REALLY speak through me!" I realised that I very strongly needed Him to speak through me if I was to speak anything at all. I went to the lectern and began disastrously, my first sentence being, "The annual Sports and Cultural meet is an annual affair."

I moved from the valleys to the dales to hit my nadir of public speaking in terms of content and delivery. I could see many of my 'friends' heads crestfallen and some people were even laughing at the mess I was making of myself.

One plea filled look at Swami and a current of inspiration jerked me alive. A new enthusiasm rang in my voice and I could not believe my ears when there was a thunderous applause three minutes later!

With gratitude I continued and the speech seemed to become a rousing success. I was applauded 4 times after that (yes, I was counting!) and when I concluded, the clapping was just one level below a standing ovation. I was very happy and felt rescued. I went to Swami and gratefully bowed at His feet for I knew it was not me

The story of the boy, who overcame fear and injury to do a carabining stunt, got me rousing applause during the speech.

who had spoken. He looked at me and asked, "Which class?" I answered, "Second year MSc Swami."

Then as I was about to rise, He called me. Looking into my eyes, He asked in Hindi, *"Tumko Pehle Kuch Nahi Diya?"* (Haven't I given you anything before?) In a flash that scene popped up in my mind's eye where I had told Him that He had given me nothing. Tears flowing down my cheek, I said, *"Swami mere paas jo bhi hain, aapne diya!"* (Swami, whatever I have with me, you have only given.)

A twinkle came in his eye. He was happy that His child who had misunderstood Him was back on the path of understanding. He then waved His hand and created a gold chain with a pendant for me. He made my head rest on His lap as He chained me to Him - forever. With tears still streaming from my eyes, I said, "Swami I don't know what to say!" He patted me on my cheeks and said, "Only Love, Love, Love, Love!" I returned back to my place.

Now I realise that "unconditional friendship" is a very tough thing. I only stated my intent but filled my head with expectations of Him. And I ended up criticising Him and not wanting to speak to Him. But He had already extended His hand of unconditional friendship to me and come what may, never left me or got angry with me. I realized that true love, instead of being the greatest binding force on earth, is actually the greatest liberating force. He was happy with me no matter what I thought or did. He had no expectations of me and still He loved me wholly. He loved me and loves me for what I am rather than for what He wants me to be. And that is because, in the ultimate analysis, He just wants me to "Be"- nothing more, nothing less.

I wish in my heart that I can become at least in part like Him and love Him to one millionth portion the way He loves me. Looking back at the beach of my life, I realise that the single set of footprints in times of crises is indeed mine. Those are the times when He taught me how to walk, always carrying Him in my heart!

He chained me for life with His love.

Chapter Twenty One

The Independence Day 'Drama' In Sri Sathya Sai's Presence

The Surprising 'Instruction'...

Turning through the pages of my diary, I come to an episode through which the Master chose to teach many lessons for life. The timing and occurrence of this episode which spanned almost a week was centred around the 57th Indian Independence Day on the 15th of August, 2004. Some of the lessons that I learnt through this episode (which I hope to remember whenever I need) are those of conflict resolution, expanding one's heart and following one's heart or inspiration.

The sequence of events are so thrilling that the writer is tempted to rush to them at the earliest. But one cannot hope to enjoy a three-course gourmet feast as fast food! Following the pattern of a three-course meal, let's start with the sizzling starters - that which sets us up for what is to follow. It started with one of my classmates, Ranganatha Raju walking beside me, as we made our way to the Institute in lines. He said, "Aravind, I had Swami's dream last night." "Oh wow! That's great and nice to hear. But why are you telling me about it?" "...because there is a message in it for you..." My ears perked up. I was very eager to listen to what Swami wanted to tell me through his dream. "It is about a drama to be staged on 15th of August..." "You mean the Independence Day drama?" It was tradition for the senior-most students of the hostel to put up a drama in the hostel on the occasion of the Indian Independence Day. That drama meant a lot for the seniors as they would showcase their best acting skills, construction skills, music skills, dancing skills - you name it. "Yes! The Independence Day drama. I think Swami wants us to stage it in Sai Kulwant hall!" "This is crazy! It has never been done before", I replied.

In a few seconds before he spoke his next line, a hundred thoughts filled my head - The I-Day drama would have many scenes from the Indian freedom movement. Those would invariably show the brutality of the British invaders and the heroic life-sacrifices of many Indian patriots. These would not be appropriate for putting up in Sai Kulwant hall (the huge public meeting hall in which Bhagawan Baba meets with the thousands that gather daily), in Swami's presence! Again, what about some of the dances and songs which had a jazzy or a 'fast' feel to them? How could we put those up in Sai Kulwant hall? The light-effects, sound effects and a hundred other effects that were possible while doing a drama in the hostel (where they had been done year after year for more than a dozen times) were not possible in Swami's *darshan* hall. The rapid flow of my thoughts was interrupted by Raju's next statement,

The true Independence Day is when one achieves 'In' dependence.

"Swami said that He has given you the theme for the drama. So, I thought it would be best if we discuss and think of how best to execute that theme." I was in a daze now. I was confused. "Are you sure that you saw Swami in your dream and He told you all this?" "Do you think I would have the courage to come and talk to you this way if I was not convinced?" "Listen Raju. I promise that Swami has not given me any theme for a drama to be put up in His presence for Independence Day. I don't know how you should proceed." "When Swami says that He has given, He has given. You have not recognised it yet. Think deeply about it and please tell me as soon as the theme gets concretised."

Resolution Of The 'Mystery' Theme

With that, we entered the assembly hall of the college where silence was a compulsory thing. I was doing some serious soul-searching throughout the prayer session. There were hardly nine days left for the Independence Day and was Swami expecting us to conjure a programme of a quality which could be put up in His presence in the *mandir*? I take Swami's dreams seriously always. And today, I also see a kind of connection between me and Raju when it comes to Swami's dreams.

A whole day passed without much luck. The next day, as I was taking a shower, a single thought kept pounding against my heart. It was saying, "In Sanskrit, 'independence' is denoted by **Swarajya**. Find the meaning of this word." This kept going on within me and it seemed as if I would not be able to do anything else unless I answered this voice. When I discovered the meaning, was I excited! Swarajya is constituted by "Swa" and "Rajya". While the former means "Self", the latter means "Rule". And here, 'Self' stands for the inner self, the Atma or God within. So, true 'independence' is when the Atma or Self rules.

Independence Therefore Is In-dependence

The way in which the inspiration had manifested, I was convinced that it was Swami who had provided the 'theme' for a drama. I rushed to Raju and told him the sequence of events. He was excited too. He was also firmly convinced that it was Swami who had provided the theme. The story flow we arrived at, was like this:

1. August 15th 1947 was the day India attained independence - freedom from the British rule - which was purely in the physical sense.

2. We have to attain the next level of independence which is freedom from the chains of poverty, corruption, immorality etc. which bind us.

3. We can be truly free only when we achieve the final level which is Swarajya or rule by the Self.

In the course of our research while making the drama and presentation we came across another amazing point. Swami refers to India as Bharat and an Indian as Bharatiya. Swami's definition, however, is so different from ours. He says,

"Bharat is the Moolasharam of Sathya, Shanti and Prema and she has been holding forth these ideals and emphasising their practice since centuries. Bharat means the land that has "rati" or attachment to "bha" or Bhagawan; it means that the people here are God-loving, not so much God-fearing. If you love God, you have to love Man also. This teaching, that Sathya is the basis of Dharma which lays down individual and social duties and obligations, and that Sathya is also the root of Prema and Shanti, is the unique feature of Bharat. Sathya is enough, no other God needs to be worshipped."

- Discourse at Bangalore, Shivaajinagar, 14-12-1963

We felt that we must mention this also. It would make the Independence Day celebrations global and universal and not restricted merely to 'Indians'!

Rough Waters...

At this point, we called a few more like-minded classmates and discussed the program. Everyone was excited and soon, a beautiful drama had taken shape. We thought that it was time to share the same with the whole class, enlist its support and start preparing for this added and new programme. We did not have the slightest idea of the opposition that we would meet! Even as we explained the concept to the class, there were protests. "We have already allocated resources (human and material) for the hostel drama. How can we accommodate this now?" "Please do not try to force 'spirituality' down people's throats! It gets nauseating. It is of no use preaching spirituality like this everywhere."

"Independence Day has been a hostel programme and a way for all the senior students to showcase their talents. Let it be that way because there is no way we can do two programmes on the same day - then justice will not be done to either of them! We can make a programme for the *mandir* later!" "Such a programme has never been done in Swami's presence. How do you think we will get the permission to do so?"

The way things went, we now had to choose between preparing for the 'traditional' hostel programme (with its 100% probability of happening) and preparing for the 'radical' *mandir* programme (with its 50% probability of happening). A vote was cast by the 120 students of the class and it was 60-40 in favour of the programme in the *mandir*.

The problem with democracy is that the majority decides everything! Though the vote said that the *mandir* programme should be planned, we had a huge 40% of the class unhappy with the decision. Instead of agreeing with the majority, they went about attempting to convince the 'opposition' about the hostel programme and increase their support-percentage! Thus it was that two programmes were being prepared simultaneously - one for the *mandir* by 60% of the class and one for the hostel by 40% of the class. (Aren't these exactly the problems in democracy!!)

Both 'parties' were racing against time to get the programmes ready. The preparations were impaired by the fact that we were a disunited class trying to achieve something that had never been done before – two programmes in the same day! The 'hostel team' suffered a handicap - most of the better actors and speakers were part of the '*mandir* team'. The '*mandir* team' was not problem-free - most of the skilled artists who would make the sets for the drama and help in the costumes were part of the 'hostel team'. We often had discussions, debates, arguments and conflicts between the two teams. But as these happened, not a word of it was allowed to leak outside the class. The teachers were not aware of this happening. Both the teams had put up their proposals to the Warden who had taken them up to the Vice-Chancellor. They were amazed at our confidence and our class' track record at putting programmes convinced them that we would be successful this time also. The Vice-Chancellor sought permission from Swami for the *mandir* programme. It was granted and we were all tensed. Though the Vice-Chancellor and the elders were praising our class, they were not aware of the severe disunity problems plaguing us. This was the setting when we began our practice on the 10th of August for programmes on the 15th of August - one in *mandir* and one in the hostel.

The Problems Increase...

Days passed this way and though in the heart of our hearts we knew that 'infighting' and 'disunity' were not the ways to prepare for two dramas, one of which would be staged in the Divine Presence. It was so ironic that we were presenting stories of unity and brotherhood while we lacked those very virtues. We were told that the Vice-Chancellor would be visiting the hostel to see our practice. He would also take a call on whether the drama had 'stuff' in it to be presented in public with Swami as the Chief Audience. This viewing could be the 'semi-final' effort for us which would decide whether we would be 'playing' the finals on the 15th of August. When we presented the drama on the morning of the 14th of August, the Vice-Chancellor, based on his wealth of experience, pointed out some 'defects' which he wanted to be rectified. This came as a big blow for us. Why? Here I list out the reasons:

1. We were opening the drama with a powerful scene in Hindi in which Bhagat Singh was the protagonist. The story was based at the time of his hanging and thus a noose had become an integral part of the scene. As mentioned earlier, we did not have many artists in our '*mandir* team'. It was with great difficulty that we had made this 'noose structure'. It was one of the only sets we had for that scene. The Vice-Chancellor felt that it would be too 'strong' and 'gruesome' to be portrayed in front of Swami. He asked for the noose to be taken away and the scene to be changed a bit.

The 'controversial' scene of the hanging of Bhagat Singh.

2. There was a very poignant scene in the drama based on a heart-rending episode during the freedom movement. A huge group of protesters seeking complete freedom are conducting a peaceful march against the British rulers. When they do not heed to the warnings, the British soldiers open fire on them. Even as the non-violent protesters fall down dead, row after row, they do not allow the Indian flag to fall. They keep passing it to the person behind. When the last protester is shot with the Indian flag in hand, he plants it into the bullet hole in his body so that it stands upright and does not 'bite the dust'. The Vice-Chancellor felt that this would again be a very brutal depiction of violence which may not be all that good in a holy gathering place. He was completely justified for, as I said before, such a drama had never been done before.

3. We wanted to conclude the programme with the National Anthem. Here, the Vice-Chancellor brought up a subtle point which we had not thought about before. It was the time when Swami had a fall and would walk 'with support'. The Vice-Chancellor said, "If you sing the National Anthem and Swami decides to stand up in spite of His condition, it would be us who are imposing it on Swami." "But Sir, we could request Swami to be seated all the while..." "I don't think we should take a chance because if He decides to stand up, then nobody can do anything about it."

That sealed matters. He told us to incorporate those changes and that he would be back again, the next day to see our drama and give a go-ahead. And the next rehearsal, he said, would be with all the sets in place too! We were all in a spot of bother. First of all, how were we to change or replace three powerful and important portions of the programme? Secondly, what sets would we show when we had none at all?

A Brave Step...

After a whole night of deliberation, we came up with a very brave plan. We would simply drop the shooting scene completely and remove the noose from the opening scene. As for the sets, we thought we would confess to the Vice-Chancellor that ours would be a 'dialogue-based' drama and the minimal sets were a way of focusing attention on the acting and dialogue-delivery (which were fantastic thanks to the sincere efforts of all concerned). As for the National Anthem, we had the bravest part of the plan. We thought that the next day morning (i.e. the 15th August), after the flag hoisting when we went to *mandir*, we would seek Swami's permission to sing it at the end of the drama. If Swami permitted us, then the Vice-Chancellor would agree too.

Before I delve into the mind-blowing and amazing happenings of the next day, let me state that the 'hostel team's' effort was unsatisfactory as well, on their drama front. They had magnificent sets ready no doubt - they had dozens of lanterns in three colours that would constitute a flag at night as the highlight of the many props they had made. However, they lacked the acting and dialogue delivery skills. There was not much 'stuff' in their presentation and they were wondering as to what they would do.

There you are then - we had two teams struggling on different fronts for putting up dramas in different venues.

The morning of the 15th of August 2004 dawned. We attended the flag hoisting ceremony at the Institute before going to *mandir* for *darshan*. Swami had already arrived and had completed the *darshan* rounds. He was in the interview room. However, when He saw that the students had arrived, He came out to take another round. Three of us were seated in the front row and we thought that this second round would be a boon for us to seek our 'National Anthem' singing chance! That was not to be however. Swami passed by us but He just told us to sit down. Thus, we could not seek any clarification nor make any prayers to Him. He went into the interview room again. We thought that the three of us should go and sit in the front of the *bhajan* hall. Since the front door there was by the side of the interview room door, we thought that we could get another chance to ask Swami about our singing if we sat there.

The Unexpected Bounty...

As we sat there, we saw that our Warden was called into the interview room. Seeing this, we got excited, "I think Swami is about to discuss our drama and so He is calling the Warden in", we told each other. In a short while however, the Warden came out of the interview room. He seemed to be frantically searching for someone. When he turned to our side, a feeling of relief wiped across his face. He came straight to us and said, "Swami wants to know the entire story of what is being portrayed in the drama today... I am not able to recollect all the details..." "Sir! Is it possible that one or two of us come in to tell the story to Swami?", I asked with a lot of excitement and a tinge of nervousness. "I think that is a good idea. Two of you can come in and tell Swami the story. The other one should ensure that all the boys taking part in the drama are assembled here, in this *bhajan* hall. We never know what Swami has in mind. In case He decides to bless all the boys, it is better that they are here."

This was simply amazing! What a turn of events and what a chance! We wanted to sit at the door so that we get a chance to speak to Him and here He was, summoning us into the interview room! The two of us, Jagdish and I, slowly entered the interview room. Swami was sitting on a sofa in the corner and seated on the floor was the Vice-Chancellor. The Warden sat down next to the Vice-Chancellor. We were still standing when Swami asked Jagdish, "What is your role?" "Swami, I am the grandfather..." "And yours?" I did not say anything for I was not acting in the drama as such. He continued, "Are you the one running away to America?" I immediately knelt before Him and told Him that the grandson is the one who wants to go to America but towards the end of the drama he has a change of heart. He stays back. I also told Him that the grandson's role was being played by someone else.

Swami smiled and told us to sit down. My heart was beating so fast and I was simply thrilled at the beautiful opportunity. Looking around, I saw that I was seated beside the Warden and Vice-Chancellor of the Institute. Where else but in God's presence could all be seated as equals? Swami was looking at the roof. He seemed lost. After about 11 seconds of silence, He began to say, (still looking at the ceiling), "There are 11 main characters in the drama. 5 of them are in the same family. There is a friend who comes in. There is Bhagat Singh. The other characters are distributed in the other parts of the drama... Right?" He looked at us. We just nodded in agreement. He had stated the beginning of our play in perfect order. We were so happy and we knew that this would be a very memorable session. What we did not know was that this interview would be the basis of many lessons for life.

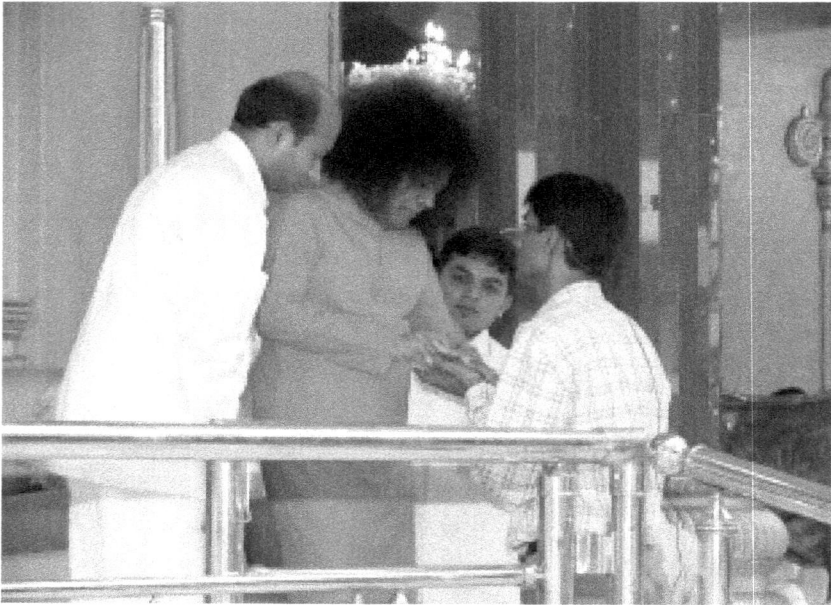

The drama behind the scenes was more dramatic than the actual drama, as the experience of R. Prashant revealed (Swami gifts him a ring in this photo).

Inspiration Is GOD...

Swami often speaks of the five mothers that we have to revere - *Dehamata* (Physical Mother), *Deshamata* (Motherland), *Bhoomata* (Mother Earth), *Gomata* (the cow), *Vedamata* (the Vedas). In the interview that followed, we got a glimpse of the importance He placed on the motherland. It showed as His great love for the patriots who had sacrificed for the nation.

Swami started with words of praise for Subash Chandra Bose, the valiant freedom fighter who was instrumental in raising the INA - Indian National Army - which has today developed into a massive army. Swami revealed his daughter was a deeply devoted lady and she even sang good *bhajans*. We were just listening with open mouths and open hearts. He praised the humility and simplicity of Rajendra Prasad, the first President of independent India. He also spoke about the excellent poetry skills that Sarojini Naidu possessed. He was also full in praise for the trio of Lala Lajpat Rai, Bal Gangadhar Tilak and Bipin Chandra Pal - popularly called Lal-Bal-Pal.

Even as he told about the trio, He asked us whether they featured in the drama. The Warden answered on our behalf and said, "Swami only certain episodes have been included due to lack of time." Swami then told Jagdish who was by my side that their names at least must be mentioned. We promised Him that we would do that. Then came the most poignant part of the interview. Swami suddenly turned to the Warden and the Vice-Chancellor and said, "People do not know the true meaning of Swaraj. They think that Swaraj means freedom from foreign rule. Swaraj is actually Swaaraaj. Swaa and Raaj." I popped up like a jack-in-the-box and in great excitement blurted out, "Swami, we are mentioning this in the drama!! We are stating that Swaa means SELF and Raaj is RULE. It is only when the SELF, ATMA or CONSCIENCE rules that we can have true freedom. True freedom is liberation from body attachment which comes from the knowledge that everyone is the spark of the Divine. And this can happen only if we follow our conscience."

Even as I completed saying it, I felt that maybe I had spoken too much. But my excitement was due to the fact that this was the same inspiration which had been the genesis of the drama - the concept of true Swaraj.

Swami was looking at me and He seemed to almost be drinking in every word I said. Then, He turned to the Warden and said, "See! The boys are very good. They quickly grasp whatever is said." This was a great revelation for me. Swami had never said anything to us. And yet, He said that we had grasped quickly whatever had been said. The concept of Swaraj had only been an inspired feeling in my heart. This proved that inspiration we feel in the heart is a way in which the Lord communicates with us. It is only a heart that has been touched by the Divine which can feel inspiration.

And to prime this inspiration, we need to enter the depths of silence.

All Problems Solved In A Trice...

As a corollary, ensure that there are things everyday which inspire you because that is the sure way of knowing that you are in touch with the Divine within. Inspiration is divine! As if adding further weight to this, Swami also began to say, "People also do not understand what Bharat is. They mistakenly think that Bharat means India..." Again, I popped up in excitement, "Swami, we are saying this too!! Bharat is a place where the human values are practiced and there is great love for the Lord. It is not a geographical entity but a value-based one. If one has true love for God and follows the five human values, one becomes a Bharatiya." Swami smiled in approval and seemed to enjoy my excitement. Again, an inspired idea had Divine approval because isn't inspiration in itself divine?

As we were speaking about the drama, we told Swami that there was a scene of Bhagat Singh which had the noose as the backdrop. We also told Him about the shooting scene which had been deemed violent and had been cancelled by the Vice-Chancellor. He heard us and then said, "Those are violent of course, but they happened in history. So, if you must portray them do so honestly. However, do not lay emphasis on the violence. Emphasise on the patriotism and love for the country." Even as these words dropped from the Divine lips, we were so thrilled! Both our jettisoned scenes were back on board now! And since Swami had stated the same in the presence of the Warden and Vice-Chancellor too, there would be no convincing needed on our part. This encouraged us both and we gently whispered to the Warden, "Sir! About the national anthem..." Now, the Warden rose on his knees and said, "Swami the boys are praying for an opportunity to sing the National Anthem in Your presence. Only they will stand up Swami...only them..."

Swami interrupted, "Why? Are not the other beings in Sai Kulwant hall also humans? They too have feelings. Let all the people stand and sing together. It will be good." We somehow controlled ourselves from jumping up with a "Yippeee". This was the reason we were seeking out Swami and He had bestowed it on us even without 'us' asking!

Unity And Love Blossom In Everyone

I remembered that the Warden had asked for all the actors to be assembled in the *bhajan* hall. It was almost half an hour since the interview had started. So I asked, "Swami, it will be nice if you speak to all the other boys of the drama too." "I will speak definitely..." Even as Swami said that, I got up to go out and call all the boys. Swami immediately stopped me and said, "Not now! Two boys are not there. I shall speak to all of them in the afternoon."

I returned to my place and the interaction continued. After a while, Swami indicated that it was time for us to leave. We went to

Him and prayed that we get a good character. He replied,
"There is no need to make your character good. You already have
good character. Ensure that nothing spoils it. Past is past. Forget it.
Be good boys." It was with great relief, joy and peace that we exited
the interview room after taking *padanamaskar*. Even as we were
exiting, He told us again to convey His blessings to all and that He
would interact with all the participants.

All the students who were part of the drama were waiting for
us to come out and tell all that had happened. In a matter of an
hour, Swami had turned us into heroes. We passed the message
around that all participants should gather in the Sai Kulwant Hall
itself after the morning session. Swami arrived for the *bhajan* session,
received Arati and retired for the morning. Soon after that, all of us
gathered.

The thrill and amazement was such that even many members
of the 'hostel drama team' gathered. I was in a very expansive and
love-filled mood. In hostel lingo, this is called AIDS (Acquiring
Intense Devotion Suddenly)! What else could I feel after such a
session with the Lord! Jagadish and I stood in the centre of the
circle as everyone gathered around us. We noticed that EXACTLY
two actors were missing! They had been practicing late night and so
had not been able to get up in the morning. Ah! What does one
speak of His omniscience and Love? We both shared all the
wonderful happenings in the interview room. We also conveyed
Swami's promise that He would interact with all of the boys. The
touch of the Lord had made us so large-hearted and loving that we
said, "There is nothing like hostel-drama and *mandir*-drama. It is all
ours. We are one. Everyone, irrespective of the drama they are in,
is welcome for the session with Swami in the afternoon."

With that, the floodgates of Love opened up suddenly. The
main members of the hostel team came up and said, "We have
made so many beautiful sets. Of what use are they if we cannot
offer them to our Lord. Swami has so much expectation of us and

is eagerly looking forward for the drama. We shall give all the sets and other things we have made for the *mandir*. You need not even worry about putting up the decorations and sets. We will do the moving and shifting. We will transport all the sets from hostel to *mandir*." We (the *mandir*-team till now) made a reciprocal promise, "We will participate in the hostel drama. Though there is very little time, immediately after the drama in the *mandir*, we shall sit and improve the plot of the hostel drama. We shall all participate in it for the hostel drama too, is ours!"

We were in tears even as we heard this. On Independence Day, we were experiencing true freedom - freedom from egotism, from rivalry, from hatred, from anger; a freedom that had liberated us into expansive love. We were able to enjoy the 'brotherhood of man under the fatherhood of God'! And all this had happened with the touch of the Lord!

There were no teams now - it was one unified class. And what joy it was to be united! The way we worked for the next three hours was simply marvellous. Everything fell in place. Everyone had smiles to share with each other. So much love had cropped up. Ah! I needed no further proof - Prem Eashwar Hai, Eashwar Prem Hai (Love is God and God is Love). By 3pm on the 15th of August 2004, all of us assembled in the *bhajan* hall of Sai Kulwant Hall. The whole class was here and we were on the verge of creating history - the first ever Independence Day programme in the Divine presence, in Sai Kulwant Hall.

As promised, Swami blessed all the participants of the
drama in the Bhajan hall, that afternoon.

The Bhajan Hall Blessings...

The whole class was inside the *bhajan* hall. The main hall in
the meanwhile had been tastefully decorated. The sets were all in
place. This drama was going to be presented LIVE! That was going
to be a challenge in itself - there were no recorded tracks. The audio-
team was to be seated along the sides of the performance area and
control all the mikes. The sets team was ready behind the scenes.
The costumes team had its task cut out in getting everyone ready in
time. There were also teams for the lights and sets movement. When
anyone sees the Taj Mahal, they exclaim about its beauty. But, they
never realise that it has a strong and mighty foundation supporting
it from below. These teams were like the foundation for the edifice
that our drama was going to be. They may not be seen or appreciated
but without them, the drama's super-structure would collapse.

Right now, all the teams had gathered in the *bhajan* hall. Soon, the *darshan* music came on and Swami arrived. Having completed His *darshan* rounds, He was entering the interview room. He saw into the *bhajan* hall and asked the student who was holding His hand as He walked, "Are these our students inside?" He nodded in agreement and Swami immediately took a diversion and came into the *bhajan* hall. What followed next was sheer bliss for all the students. He enquired into many boys as to what role they were playing in the drama. He enquired about the INA cadets, Subash Chandra Bose and several other characters. He suddenly asked, "What is Subash Chandra Bose's daughter's name?" None of us knew. He smiled and said that she was greatly devoted to God and she sings *bhajans* well. Blessed indeed was she that Swami remembered her twice on the same day I thought. Swami pointed to one of the students and said, "See, this boy's face is exactly like Subash Chandra Bose. He should have been made that character. The face should match." We just nodded for there was not much we could do immediately. I promised, "Swami, next time, if we portray Subash Chandra Bose, we shall use him only for the role."

The topic continued about Subash Chandra Bose as Swami continued to interact with other actors. Many took *namaskar*. One of the students mentioned, "Swami, Subash Chandra Bose wrote a letter to his mother stating that he wished to achieve complete freedom. Such a freedom would ensure that he would never be bound by time, space or body again." Swami nodded appreciatively. Many more interactions took place which I do not recollect vividly. One I remember because it concerns me. Since Swami had asked me whether I was the lad 'running away to America', I pointed out to the boy, R.Prashant, doing that role and said, "Swami this is the boy going to America." Swami looked deeply at him. There was silence. I did not know whether what I had done was right. Immediately, I said, "Swami, but his grandfather convinces him and he stays back." Swami just smiled.

He moved ahead and cut the cake that had been baked specially for the occasion by a few members of the class. He lit the candle atop the cake too. Looking at the clock, Swami asked as to how long the drama would take. The Warden said that it was about an hour. He blessed us all to do well and told us to start moving out. "I shall soon come there," He said.

As we were moving out towards the performance area, the Warden called me aside and said, "Before you start the programme, make an announcement..." "What should I announce Sir?" "Say that the senior most students of the Institute are putting up a drama and then say the drama's name." It suddenly struck me that our drama had not yet been christened. On my way to the mike, I named it, "From independence to Swarajya" because I thought that it would highlight the difference between independence as we know it from the rule of the Self.

The drama went on very well. It was gripping and Swami was enjoying every bit of it. The Bhagat Singh scene, the shooting scene and the scene involving the grandfather and grandson were all good. One good thing was that the grandfather, based on the input from Swami, incorporated an extemporaneous dialogue wherein he mentioned Lal-Bal-Pal. Swami smiled and looked very proud. All the dialogues were delivered live, songs were sung live and the background music was provided live.

Thrilled members of the drama troupe with the Divine Director.

A 'Drama' Of Many Dimensions...

Singing the National Anthem in the presence of the "Bharata Bhagya Vidata" (dispenser of Bharat's destiny). As we concluded and came in for the final formation, Swami descended from the stage and came in our midst. He seemed so happy and was beaming with pride. He materialised a ring for the 'grandfather' who had transformed his grandson. He materialised rings for two more actors. And then, finally, He materialised another ring for the 'grandson' who had decided to stay back in India and not go abroad!! There were tears of joy in the eyes of the 'grandson' or so I thought. It was only later that I came to know that these were tears of awe and gratitude as well. The 'grandson's' story was fascinating to say the least. I must mention it here. It was in 2001 that he happened to attend a discourse by Swami at Brindavan in Bangalore. In that discourse Swami spoke strongly against abandoning one's motherland and going abroad. He said that one must serve one's motherland. The lad, R.Prashant, had been planning for a bright overseas career. Hearing the discourse, he decided that, come what may, he would stay in India and work for its uplift. This was a story he had told none and so he was amazed at the role he got to play in the drama. As he heard his 'grandfather' inspire him to stay back and serve the motherland, he felt deja vu. And Swami had patted him, materialising a ring for him in appreciation.

Today, R.Prashant has started many rural initiatives as his bit to serve his motherland. One of these ventures, Sai Seva, is a rural BPO that is based in Puttaparthi itself. These are the stories which constitute the drama behind a drama! Swami went up on the stage again. He said that He would grant group photos. This time, another marvellous gesture was seen.

All the actors spontaneously signalled to the sets team, costumes team and the audio team saying, "You first." The actors felt that it was time for the others to receive their fair share of the Lord's physical proximity. At this point, Swami even cast a mini-test. He said that He would grant photos to only 4-5 groups. In spite of that, the 'background teams' were allowed to go. In fact, after those teams had their pictures taken, Swami decided to leave. None of the actors had any sad feelings! Swami said that such dramas must travel all through the nation. He said that He was very happy and He retired for the day. Everyone was happy all around. With Swami it is always like that - a win-win-win-win situation where there is no loser!

Before I forget, let me mention that we returned to the hostel triumphantly. With renewed vigour and enthusiasm we worked for the drama there. The drama in the hostel too turned out to be unforgettable and brilliant. The highlight was the hoisting of the Indian Tricolor made completely of oil lamps and lampshades. The flag measured an impressive 15 feet by 10 feet! There was a standing ovation for the performance.

That was how the Divine Drama had been enacted. The two dramas on stage that day had such a powerful, poignant, message-filled and unforgettable drama behind them. A drama that the Divine Director staged so that His children learn unity, love, inspiration, peace, harmony and more than anything else, the fact that nobody who ever places faith in the Lord is ever let down. God brings men into deep waters not to drown them, but to cleanse them. That was another takeaway.

Chapter Twenty Two

A Rose Bud Offered To God

Another Day At Prasanthi Nilayam

It was one of those days when speakers were scheduled to deliver talks before Bhagawan Baba's divine discourse in the Sai Kulwant hall at Prasanthi Nilayam, Puttaparthi. Everyone began to assemble in the hall from 1:30pm itself for the programme that would begin at about 4:00pm. The front blocks, as always, were occupied by the students. When Swami arrived for His *darshan* rounds, the hall was an epitome of discipline and devotion as more than 10,000 people drank in the nectarine bliss of simply seeing Him.

Baba arrived on the dais and the proceedings began with the mighty chanting of the Vedic hymns by students from the Sri Sathya Sai University. Ten minutes later, the first speaker for the evening was introduced. As he walked out to speak, he carried a little rose bud with him. Undoubtedly, that would be his offering to Swami before he took blessings and proceeded to the lectern. That interaction lasted a few moments and soon, the speaker was standing before the microphone delivering his speech.

Seated at the centre of the dais, Swami picked up the rose bud that had been offered to Him.

The Bud 'Grows'

At first, He began to simply look at the little bud nestled in His hands. A sweet little smile blossomed on His face. Then, ever so gently, He began to open the closed petals of the rose flower. It had to be done slowly else the petal would get disconnected from the main stalk. He held the stalk in His left hand and was opening up the petals, one by one, with the fingers of His right hand.

The green, leafy sepals that were located at the bottom of the flower too opened. As the speaker continued to speak, it was an amazing sight to see Swami so engrossed in this 'gardening' task! The stalk of the flower had a few thorns which He broke off. That was quite amazing because the thorns are pretty strongly glued to the stalk. Once the few thorns were stripped away, He continued with the act of opening the petals. And again, the strength of His fingers gave way to their tenderness and gentleness.

It took about fifteen minutes for the talk to conclude. In those fifteen minutes, the rose bud that had been offered to Swami underwent a complete transformation. It was no longer a bud but a fully blossomed rose flower sans its thorns. As the speaker concluded, there was a thunderous applause. Swami smiled and there was a look of satisfaction on His face. For an observer who had been seeing the metamorphosis of the rose bud, it felt as if the applause was meant for Swami who had done something beautiful - blossomed a bud into a flower. And Swami seemed to simply smile it away in divine humility.

Naturally so, because day in and day out, He is engaged in exactly this. Accepting the lives that have been offered to Him as tiny buds and making them blossom with His divine, transforming touch!

Whatever be the objective that one wishes to achieve in life, the world believes in starting early. A child is enrolled into an arts class, gymnastics lessons, kindergarten or music at ages like 3-4. That is considered great and wonderful. However, when it comes to spirituality, the thought is to take it up after retirement at age 60!

Spirituality is not to be confused with religion. Spirituality is a way of life where one keeps in mind the impermanence of the world and everything in it.

Thus, it makes sense that one desirous of taking up spirituality should also get into it young. That was exactly what Swami told a student very poignantly in an interview -

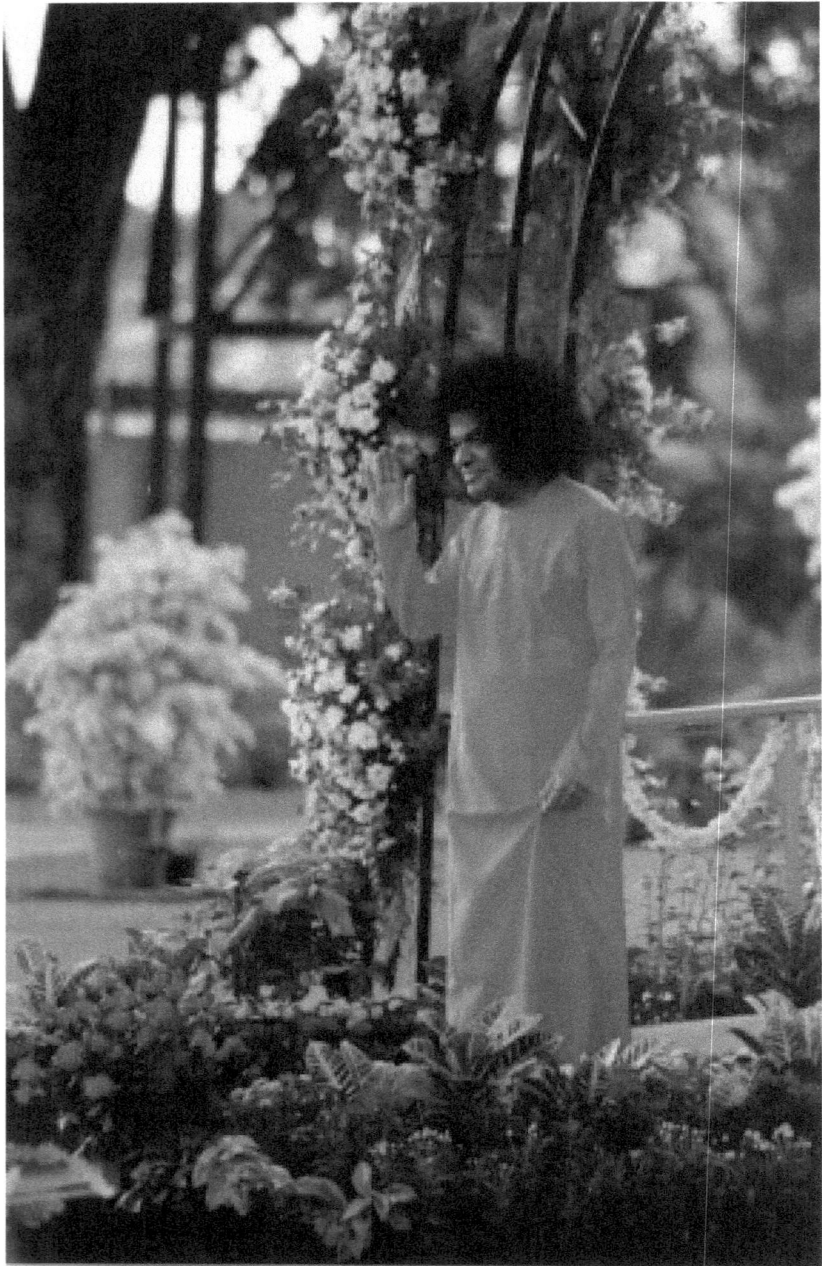

It is the touch of the Master that blossoms every bud.

"If anyone offers their love to God in their youth, they earn the right to demand from the Lord anything, anytime. Youth is the most sacred time in life which should be offered to the Lord."

An Excerpt From A Discourse

We offer food to God on a clean plantain leaf. But today we have to enquire what type of food is offered and to whom. The human body is the plantain leaf, the heart of man is the sacred vessel and virtues, and sacred feelings and good conduct are like the sacred food items. But to whom are these being offered? These are being offered to demons of evil qualities, wicked feelings such as anger, hatred, and jealousy. The food that is eaten and left over by these demons of hatred, anger, and jealousy is being offered to God. That is why people today are the victims of restlessness, difficulties, sorrows, and misery.

Young age is like a delicious fruit. You should offer this sweet and delicious fruit to God. It is not possible to worship God after your retirement in old age, when your body becomes weak, the sense organs lose their power, and the mind becomes feeble. Start early, drive slowly, reach safely. Start praying to God right from the early age. If you do not undertake sacred actions when your physical and mental faculties are strong, then when will you perform them? What can you do when the sense organs have lost all their power?

How can you think of God when you become a decrepit old man? Offer the fragrant flowers of your mind and heart to God with total faith at a young age, when your body is strong and sense organs are powerful. This is the true naivedyam (food offering) that you have to offer to God. But people today do not make such offerings. When their senses become weak after indulging in all sorts of sensual pleasures, they offer them to God like offering leftover food.

Divine Discourse On 16th July 1996

Chapter Twenty Three

Dreams Of Swami Are True

It was in 2006 that the Yajur Mandir, the Divine Residence of Bhagawan Sri Sathya Sai Baba got sanctified with His touch for the first time. Somehow, my mind flashed back to the wonderful happenings of that day. It was another instance that showed that when it concerns Swami, dreams and reality are no different. The episode took place as the Hindu year Vyaya began on the 30th of March 2006.

Swami seemed excited like a child about the inauguration of the new residence. Even as I type this sentence, my heart takes a detour. Though I know that it has nothing to do with 'dreams about Swami' being true, I cannot help but move along that route. Forgive this detour and listen to what my heart has to say.

The Lord's Living Quarters

From my limited knowledge, this would be the first time that Swami would be getting a decent sized room on top. Swami has always been liberal when it comes to comforts of the devotees. As far as His own comforts were concerned, notwithstanding the prayers and pleadings of a thousand devotees, He stayed in a small room that measured hardly 10 feet by 5 feet. His cot, a table and chair were the only furnishings and a fan was the only companion against the harsh Puttaparthi heat. No TV, no gadgets - absolutely none of the items that any one of us consider necessary. It was only Swami and Himself. His room above the Prashanti *bhajan mandir* led out to a stairway and this stairway was so narrow that Swami fitted on it only due to His petite frame. Once off the stairway, His privacy ended and the interview room opened out in the ground floor. Here, the environs were so different. A soft carpet on the floor, an exhaust fan, good lights and a modern fan! After all, wasn't it for His dear devotees?

In 1993, He shifted residence to a room in the upper portion of the Poornachandra Auditorium. He again did not allow for any luxuries and comforts. His residence, in fact was a modified 'green room'! Again, the veranda and public hall where He met devotees were well furnished but he did not allow the same to be done to His room! Ah Lord! You never ever cared for yourself. All the while your thoughts and concern was about the devotees only. The small bathroom light in the residence was most used for He sat there late in the nights at times and early in the mornings reading the letters that His devotees offered. He used His human frame like a candle, burning away to shed light for everyone!

Ugadi, 2006 – When He moved into His new residence, Yajur Mandir.

Scheduling A Programme For Ugadi

After pleadings, prayers, letters, requests and penance, He had agreed for Yajur mandir. All of us students and the devotees were happy. We were excited for we felt that by convincing Swami to move into Yajur Mandir, we were doing at least something for

Him! And Swami, on His part, seemed to be mirroring our excitement. When Swami gets excited about something, everyone shares in it! And so, a host of programmes were planned for Ugadi 2006. The students had a Band programme along with the *Nadaswaram* prepared for the occasion. This was a period of time when Swami had encouraged us students to put up programmes after programmes - a time when I had experienced the most poignant events of my life. And so, a group of us students, decided to put up a programme.

The programmes we prepared those days used to be a medley of many things - songs, speeches, short skits, demonstrations and role-plays. Swami seemed to enjoy them so much that whenever we sought His permission to put up a programme, He would instantly agree. On some occasions, we had even come prepared with a programme to *mandir* and as Swami moved during *darshan*, had asked Him, "Swami we have a programme ready". Swami had made us put up a programme immediately! In fact, it is with some pride that I say this - our batch was partly responsible for the inspiration that many districts and states derived to start putting up regular programmes in Sai Kulwant hall. Before 2005-2006, programmes were never held with such frequency! What beautiful days those were... but I shall reserve that for another story.

Coming to the point, any occasion in the *mandir* was reason for us to celebrate for we would prepare a programme to be put up in front of Him. This time, there came a 'hitch'. The devotees from Andhra Pradesh had prepared a programme for Ugadi for it is the New Year Day in the state. That was not the hitch. The hitch was that the Warden called us and said,(("See, so many devotees from Andhra Pradesh have come prepared with a music programme. You boys get so many chances to put up programmes. (The years 2005-2006 saw us put up almost sixteen programmes in His presence!) So, give up Ugadi."

We were disappointed. When it comes to Swami, how much ever one gets, one is not satisfied! "Sir! Let Swami decide that. We shall also prepare a programme. Whomsoever Swami wants, will put up the programme." "If Swami sees you boys, He will definitely give you the chance and that will deprive those devotees of their chance. So, you should not interfere this time." "Sir! Please don't do this. Swami loves all equally and whatever He does is for our good..." "Think that this is Swami telling you through me..." He smiled as he said that. The tug-of-war went on. Finally, a midway solution was reached - we could prepare for a programme but we would have to sit for *darshan* in whites.

Whenever we had a programme ready, we would wear costumes or at least a color *kurta*. That was our method of indicating to Swami (as if He needed it) that we had a programme ready. Swami invariably would call one of us and ask, "What is up?" We would then detail Him about the programme and begin it. In that light, this ban on 'colored costumes' put us at a disadvantage.

"Sir! How will we indicate to Swami?" He smiled again and repeated our line back to us, "Swami loves all equally and whatever He does is for our good..." Accepting that, we began our preparations in full gusto. We had only two days to get a programme going and we began in right earnest. We broke down the programme into speaking parts, acting parts and singing parts and assigned them to different talented champions. Within a day, a nice programme had been whipped up and we practiced it for the whole day and night.

Should We Or Shouldn't We?

We had been informed that Swami was hosting all of us students for a magnificent lunch in the Poornachandra Auditorium on the occasion of the 'house-warming' ceremony of Yajur Mandir. 29th of March was a Wednesday and we came to know that for the next day, Swami wanted only a short morning programme. He wanted all of us to be early in the auditorium for lunch. The thought of feeding His children seemed to have excited Him. This combined with the fact that the Band, the Nadaswaram and the Andhra state organization had prepared programmes, acted as a dampener for us. We wondered whether we were being too greedy in wanting to put up a programme. So, as we met for the final practice on 29th night, we were a set of doubtful faces. The next day was going to be a big and busy day. Was it worth the effort to keep practicing the whole night and end up drowsy in the morning - all for our greed of putting a programme in His presence? Not able to get an answer, we resorted to a method that has been used with Swami for decades - the toss! Yes! We went to His picture in the altar and asked, "Swami please tell us whether we will be required to put a programme tomorrow morning?" When we tossed the chits, the answer came - "NO". We all just dispersed and went to bed early.

The Efficiency Of Using 'Chits'/'Toss' With Faith

If you thought that we were crazy to do this 'tossing', wait till you hear the story of my classmate. Another little detour here to help the flow of the story! It was in the summer of 2007. There was news that Swami would be leaving for Kodaikanal anytime soon. When news of a Kodaikanal trip came to our ears, we students would immediately polarise into three categories. The first were those who had received some sort of intimation from Swami that they were also in the entourage. They would spend all the time in preparing physically, mentally and spiritually for the trip. The second were those who had made up their mind to go home during the vacations. They would concentrate on getting as much as possible of Swami before they would leave for their homes for a lovely vacation. The third were those who were hopeful of being selected for the Kodaikanal trip in the days leading to Swami's actual departure from Puttaparthi.

About thirty of us were in this third category! Being in the third category was challenging in ways more than one. If selected, it was joy supreme and the wait would have 'fructified.' If not selected, then one had to make hurried bookings to leave for home. Being the vacation time, all train bookings would be full. Thus, many of us would have to estimate a probable date of Swami's departure and make a booking as a back-up!

Swami left for Kodaikanal on 26th of April that year. And this friend of mine, who was with us in the 'third' group started packing all his luggage. "Hey! How are you going home?" I asked him. "I have a train tonight." "Wow! How did you get reservation for tonight?" "I had booked a month earlier. So it was no big deal." "That was pretty lucky! You booked so perfectly! Swami leaves in the morning and you leave for home at night." "That was no luck. I did what Swami told me to do." "Swami told you to book your tickets for the 26th? How?" "Through chits..."

The 'chits' method is a variant of the 'toss'. You write two options on two different pieces of paper and throw them before Swami. Pick one and follow it is the guidelines. I was wondering how this guy got answer through the chits. "How did you do it?" "Well", he began "I was sure that Swami would leave in April. I just knew it. So, I took 30 chits of paper and wrote dates from 1st to 30th. I tossed all thirty in front of His picture and picked one. It was 26th. So I booked tickets for the 26th of April." Was I dumbstruck! Now you will appreciate why we just agreed to the result of the toss and went to bed at night on the 29th of March 2006.

Change In Plans

That night was a restful and uneventful sleep. There were no dreams. We woke up in the morning to the New Year according to the Telugu and Kannada calendars. We got ready and went to the mandir. It was a Thursday. The mandir bore a festive look and in the background we could see the Yajur Mandir standing in all grandeur and majesty, awaiting the Lord to make a formal entry. Four bands and two music groups waited in readiness to perform in the Divine presence.

Swami made a royal entry in a specially made Lamborghini car which had His seat in the front and the driver's seat behind. He

Swami's presence in Kulwant Hall
on Ugadi morning was very brief.

was in a yellow robe and everyone gasped in joy and exclamation. Swami completed the *darshan* round and even as He entered the portico, asked for Arati. Arati was given instantly after the *darshan* round, even as the *darshan* music was on! So, there was no other performance in the morning. Swami told all of us, "Come there! A feast awaits you!"

He was so happy and that made us happy.

Nothing needs to be said about the inauguration and the lunch that followed. It was a lovely event and the happenings of the morning are recorded separately. In brief, however, here it is. Professors, Heads of the departments as well as doctors and other special guests were seated inside the annex building to the new house, where on the ground floor there is a huge open hall. Swami first entered this annex and blessed everyone and supervised the serving of the food there before He proceeded to the Poornachandra auditorium. The boys had prepared a cake for Him which He cut and made all of them happy. He went up and down the aisle raising His hands many times to bless one and all, and interacted with many people before He retired to His 'new' abode.

Members of the Anantapur brass band are joyous at the opportunity to dine in His presence, on Ugadi.

After a happy morning session, we all returned to the hostel with our hearts and stomach filled to the brim. Our students 'programming' group was happy that we had followed the 'toss' decision. Looking back, it felt so perfect and nice. So, with great satisfaction, we lay on our respective beds and zoomed into the dream world. And then, I had the dream.

The Dream

In the dream Swami sent for us students asking us for the programme. I was in a state of shock. We had not been expecting this. And so, in the dream, I rush to the others and wake them from sleep telling that Swami was expecting us to put up a programme in the *mandir*. I woke up in the hostel room. The time was 1:40pm. I rushed out and woke up everyone telling them Swami wanted us to put up a programme. Everyone was taken aback and I told them all about my dream. "But the toss said that there was no need of us to prepare the programme... you remember?" Now, I was in a fix. How could the toss have gone wrong? It was then that another boy said, "In the toss we asked Swami whether there would be our programme in the morning. That does not rule out the chances of the programme in the evening!" With that realization, we all went ahead with the preparations in all seriousness.

An Amazing Sequence Of Events

In the evening, when we told the Warden about this fresh development, he also seemed to be in a fix because the programme by the Andhra state organization had been 'agreed' to. He agreed for us to sit in the front lines. But he still stuck to his guns about none of us wearing costumes or colour clothes. We agreed (what choice did we have anyway?) and proceeded to the *mandir*. We had prayers in our hearts. I was a bit tense. Everyone had prepared for the programme based on my dream. I was constantly trying to remind myself that it was not my dream but His dream actually! Swami arrived for *darshan* and came to the stage after completing His rounds. As He sat on the chair, He beckoned to us who were sitting in the first line. Two of us rushed up the stage and kneeled at His feet. He asked what the programme was. Even as I began telling about the content of our programme joyously, He asked, "Music programme?" I understood that He was referring to the programme by the Andhra state devotees. So I turned around and beckoned to the organisers of that programme. I told Swami that they would be performing. As they came to the stage, I slowly moved down and sat in my place. I was wondering as to what was happening but was happy that I got a chance to speak to Him.

"Maybe that is only the 'programme' - a reward for all the efforts." I thought as the others began to ask me about what Swami had said. In the meanwhile, Swami was blessing the dozen or so people who had moved up the stage. He received flowers and saw the cards that had been made. He spoke to many of them and gave *padanamaskar* to all of them. The whole thing took about 3-4 minutes and then all the organizers moved down the stage. Swami then called the Vice-Chancellor of the University and told him to announce the programme for the evening. The VC came to the lectern and began the announcement. It simply took our breath away. He said, (the gist is here)

"Today evening, Swami has blessed the senior students of the Institute to present us with an Ugadi programme. They will now begin the programme immediately." He looked at us and told us to begin.

Were we shocked! The singers were given the mikes and quickly the Omkaram began. Even as we started, Swami called the VC to Him and seemed to be scolding him for getting Him wrong. The VC was offering to redo the announcement and Swami was telling him something more. I thought that maybe the VC had made a mistake in the announcement. Maybe, Swami wanted the other programme. And so, as the 3 Aums were complete, we stopped completely.

Finally, it was the students, who put up the programme for Ugadi evening.

At that time, Swami looked at us, smiled and said, "Continue". He also told the Vice-Chancellor to sit. And that was it!

We performed for almost forty minutes after that. At the end of our programme, Swami was so happy that He decided to deliver His Divine Discourse!

As far as I was concerned, this was another among the many confirmations that I received that Swami in the dream is as real as Swami in reality. This reminds one of King Janaka's classic, "Is this real or that real?" By the way, just to complete the circle, I must say that the devotees from Andhra Pradesh got their chance to put the programme up in the Divine Presence on the 31st of March - the next day!

What more need to be said about Swami's dreams being true?

Chapter Twenty Four

Seek God And The Rest Will Be Conferred Upon Thee

The Story Of The Dharma Programme

Swami often gives us the example of a fruit hanging on a tree. Man sees the shadow of the fruit and attempts to grasp it. He obviously does not get the fruit. But if he makes an effort to climb the tree and pluck the fruit, the shadow too will automatically be in his grasp. With that, Swami says when one seeks the Lord, the world, which is merely the Lord's shadow, is also obtained. Seek the Lord and everything will be yours. Please the Lord and the whole world will be pleased with you. I experienced this aspect through a very flustering yet educative experience. The episode of the Dharma programe dates back to the 10th of June in 2004.

It was the beginning of a new academic year and we were all thrilled to be back in Swami's physical presence. The previous year, Swami had encouraged the senior students to put up programmes in His divine presence. We had the opportunity to put up a few programmes and were very thrilled at this opportunity. We hoped that the new academic year could begin with a programme so that the fest could continue and many students would get a chance to imbibe Swami's teachings and also get the chance of interacting with Him at a physical level. Okay. So who is this 'we' that am referring to so constantly? 'We' were the students of the final year postgraduate class.

Swami had just returned from Brindavan, Bangalore. During His two-month-long stay at Whitefield ashram, He had granted many Trayee sessions to the students. Some of us were present during those sessions. Towards the end of the holidays, we noticed that

Swami seemed to lay a lot of emphasis on 'Dharma' in all His talks and interactions at Trayee Brindavan. And so, when we sat together to think of preparing a programme, we felt that we should do something that focuses on Dharma.

Problems And Solutions

There were two problems with this proposition:

1. Dharma is not an easy topic to discuss. It is universal yet very intricate. The way it is understood varies from person to person.

2. Since it was just the beginning of the academic year, the various 'self-reliance' departments that are run by the students had not yet started. This meant that there would not be much help when it came to costumes, sets and making a card for the programme.

We solved these problems as follows:

1. We would read Swami's book, "Dharma Vahini" and stick to the meanings and interpretations present in it.

2. Our programme would be mostly talk based which would not require sets or costumes. We would have about 5-6 speakers conducting the whole programme.

So, we began reading the Dharma Vahini in right earnest and tried to digest the profound message that lay in it. Within a day, we had prepared something substantial and it was on the 10th of June when we went to the Warden to inform him that we had a programme ready to be presented before Swami. Immediately, he said, "Today is the day of *Ashtami*. We usually do not begin anything on such a day. Why don't we wait for another good day to begin the *mandir* programmes for the year?"

We did not debate that for we knew it was true. We all went to the *mandir* without any expectation or any prayer too! We had got inspired and put in efforts. Well, if God's plans were otherwise, so be it. That was our attitude.

The Happenings On That Day...

Swami granted *darshan* in the golf-cart those days. The Veda chanting was on and Swami took a complete round of the ladies' and gents' areas. The 'wheel-sofa' on which Swami sat was brought to the stage. Swami was smiling when He came. The six of us were sitting in the front (just in case) and seeing Swami smile, we felt so happy. Within fifteen minutes of His arrival, Swami looked to His left where the Vice-Chancellor, Sri S.V. Giri was seated. He called him and asked him whether there was any programme by the students. Were we surprised! Swami had not been 'told' about our preparations. But does anyone need to tell Swami anything?

The Vice-Chancellor looked at the Warden because he was not aware of any programme. The Warden went to Swami and said, "Swami, today is Ashtami. Not a good day to start programmes." Swami seemed to agree to him and continued sitting. However, after a while, He called the Warden again and posed the same question, "Is there a programme today?" Going by his previous experience with Swami, the Warden repeated his answer, "Swami today is Ashtami." Swami nodded and sent him back. After a few minutes, Swami directly asked us, "Is there a programme today?" The Warden understood that there seemed to be some change in plans. He went to Swami and told Him, "Swami there is a programme ready. Only that, since it is Ashtami, I was hesitant to say." Swami now called us to Him. He asked us what our programme was about. "Swami, it is about Atma Dharma and Para Dharma." (We did not tell Him that it was not exactly a programme of songs, dramas, skits and dances but a programme of speeches alone!) Swami seemed so eager. He said, "Go ahead! Start your programme."

"Why Fear When I Am Here."

Swami often tells us, "When you have the Lord's *anugraha* (Grace) what can the *navagraha* (planetary influences) ever do to you?" That seemed the case now. The day might have been a 'bad one' to begin endeavours. But once Swami says, what can ever affect?

The common belief is that God is the eternal witness of our actions. We keep doing things which He keeps watching. But these are times when I have felt the opposite - that God is the only doer and all of us are mere witnesses! He does. We can only witness and marvel! And thus, we took the two microphones of the Veda chanting group and began the programme. As I said before, it was only talk, talk and more talk!

Twenty minutes through the programme, as I stood up to speak for a second time, I saw that the whole audience seemed to be getting bored. It was as if the audience was simply waiting for the programme to finish. As I spoke, I turned to either side. I realised that it was a case of people tolerating me simply because Swami was tolerating me. I felt so foolish. Words that were flowing out of my mouth got stuck! I began to stammer a bit. Even as I 'heard' what I was speaking, I wondered whether there was even the slightest conviction in my voice. It was as if I was parroting in public. I felt my legs go a bit wobbly and a steep drop in confidence.

I turned to see Swami sitting behind. Ah! What a reassuring smile He gave! It was wonderful to know that Swami was 'behind' me! And this experience of mine was common across the other speakers too. Everyone felt that the audience was only tolerating us. We were feeling that Swami had so eagerly and graciously given an opportunity and we had let Him down so badly. We wanted to just stop the programme there and, like the little fish going to the feet of the fisherman who cast the net to save itself from being trapped in the net he had flung, we wanted to simply rush to Swami's feet. "This must be the negative effect of *Ashtami* acting on us." "Maybe we should have agreed to Warden and just shut up." "Swami placed so much faith in us. We have let Him down." "Only Swami is smiling. Everyone else is frowning. Our teachers too look so disappointed. What are we doing??"

These were the hushed whispers going on between us participants. Forty minutes later, I got the chance to end our agony with the final module of the programme. On the spot, I concluded with a prayer, "Swami. Dharma is a very glorious concept. We know nothing of it. Please enlighten us so that we can imbibe it in our daily life."

"When everything fails, seek refuge at His feet."
That was what we followed after the disastrous programme.

With that, I sat down and all of us were looking at Swami alone. There was no applause. A few claps here and there, mostly out of charity for the efforts made! There was absolute silence and as we looked at Swami for solace, He smiled at us. He called the six of us to Him and asked, "What did you speak?"

This was something that we had been waiting for. "Swami, we do not know what we spoke. We tried our best and spoke whatever little we understood." Swami smiled. He seemed so happy! Swami always places emphasis and gives importance to the efforts over the results. That is the nature of God.

Swami then did something beyond our wildest imagination. He waved His hand and created *vibhuti* for all of us, in full public view! Immediately, there was a resounding applause. That was not all. He called the Vice-Chancellor and told him, "These boys have so beautifully understood Dharma. If everyone understands it like them, it will be good."

That statement immediately redeemed us in the eyes of all the teachers too! In fact, we got many congratulatory messages for the 'wonderful programme' done. But we were wise enough to know that all the credit was to Swami alone. Swami was happy with our programme and the whole world was happy with us! We wanted to please Swami and unknowingly, we had got our priority right. By His Grace, we had gone for the fruit instead of its shadow!

We felt such gratitude towards Swami. We had been saved exactly like that little fish which took refuge at the feet of the fisherman who cast the net! The message we learnt that day was so straight and simple -

Do everything to please God. And realise that whatever you are doing, when offered to God, becomes His responsibility. So do not get elated by praise or get depressed with blame. Offer it wholeheartedly to Him. It keeps one karma-free as any offering made to God becomes perfect simply because it has been offered wholeheartedly to Him!

www.ingramcontent.com/pod-product-compliance
Lightning Source LLC
Chambersburg PA
CBHW060620070426
42446CB00052B/2789